RADIAL ARM SAW
BASICS

Roger W. Cliffe

Sterling Publishing Co., Inc.   New York

Metric Equivalents

INCHES TO MILLIMETRES AND CENTIMETRES

MM—millimetres   CM—centimetres

Inches	MM	CM	Inches	CM	Inches	CM
⅛	3	0.3	9	22.9	30	76.2
¼	6	0.6	10	25.4	31	78.7
⅜	10	1.0	11	27.9	32	81.3
½	13	1.3	12	30.5	33	83.8
⅝	16	1.6	13	33.0	34	86.4
¾	19	1.9	14	35.6	35	88.9
⅞	22	2.2	15	38.1	36	91.4
1	25	2.5	16	40.6	37	94.0
1¼	32	3.2	17	43.2	38	96.5
1½	38	3.8	18	45.7	39	99.1
1¾	44	4.4	19	48.3	40	101.6
2	51	5.1	20	50.8	41	104.1
2½	64	6.4	21	53.3	42	106.7
2	76	7.6	22	55.9	43	109.2
3½	89	8.9	23	58.4	44	111.8
4	102	10.2	24	61.0	45	114.3
4½	114	11.4	25	63.5	46	116.8
5	127	12.7	26	66.0	47	119.4
6	152	15.2	27	68.6	48	121.9
7	178	17.8	28	71.1	49	124.5
8	203	20.3	29	73.7	50	127.0

Library of Congress Cataloging-in-Publication Data

Cliffe, Roger W.
    Radial arm saw basics / Roger W. Cliffe.
        p.   cm.
    Includes index.
    ISBN 0-8069-7218-1
    1. Radial saws.   2. Woodwork.   I. Title.
    TT186.C54   1991
    684'.083—dc20   90-20004
                                               CIP

10 9 8 7 6 5 4 3 2

Copyright © 1991 by Roger W. Cliffe
Published by Sterling Publishing Company, Inc.
387 Park Avenue South, New York, NY 10016
Distributed in Canada by Sterling Publishing
% Canada Manda Group, P.O. Box 920, Station U
Toronto, Ontario, Canada M8Z 5P9
Distributed in Great Britain and Europe by Cassell PLC
Villiers House, 41/47 Strand, London WC2N 5JE, England
Distributed in Australia by Capricorn Ltd.
P.O. Box 665, Lane Cove, NSW 2066
Manufactured in the United States of America
All rights reserved

Sterling ISBN 0-8069-7218-1

Contents

INTRODUCTION

The radial arm saw can be a valuable and versatile workshop aid. It can be used to make different types of rip cut, mitre cut, and cross cut, to cut dadoes, rabbets, chamfers, bevels and lap joints, and even to drill and sand. *Radial Arm Saw Basics* supplies all the information beginners need to efficiently and safely use this power tool to its fullest advantage.

The information presented in the following pages was developed through my years of experience as a cabinetmaker and woodworking teacher. It is safety-oriented, and guides the reader step by step through all aspects of radial arm saw use. The first chapter explores the types of saw available, all their parts and controls, and the accessories that can be used with them. Chapter 2 examines the variety of different blades that can be used with the saw, and explains how to determine which one is the most efficient in a particular situation. Following is a chapter on safety that focuses on both general workshop safety guidelines and specific cutting

procedures and reveals the unsafe practices that can lead to an accident.

With this basic core of information firmly established, Chapters 4 and 5 clarify and illustrate step by step the proper way to set up the saw, and then the many cutting techniques possible with the machine. Chapter 6 shows how to properly adjust and maintain the machine so that it cuts properly. Chapter 7, the final chapter, supplies several useful accessories such as push sticks, featherboards, and mitring jigs, and a picture-frame project on which you can test your newly developed skills.

This book has been designed to guide you through the essentials of radial arm saw use and to whet your interests in this popular tool. For those who would like to pursue more advanced techniques and projects, consult *Radial Arm Saw Techniques* (Sterling Publishing Company, 387 Park Avenue South, New York, New York 10016).

Roger Cliffe

Chapter I

EXPLORING THE RADIAL ARM SAW

Historical Overview

The radial arm saw is an American invention. It was invented by Raymond E. DeWalt in 1922. This original saw was the model used for production, which began two years later.

The radial arm saws available today are very different from the original one. (See Illus. 1-1.) Many modifications have been made to improve the machine, which is now being manufactured all over the world.

Carpenters were the first woodworkers to reap the benefits of the radial arm saw. Before its invention, they found it difficult to handle large lumber on a table saw. With a radial arm saw, the wood remained stationary while the blade made a controlled cut. This made rafter cutting—the cutting of large framing stock—much safer, more accurate, and less fatiguing. Carpenters soon built jigs and fixtures that increased the saw's versatility.

Today, many cabinetmakers and home woodworkers also favor the radial arm saw. It can do the work of a saw, a boring machine (Illus. 1-2), or disc and spindle sanders (Illus. 1-3), while taking up very little floor space. Few machines possess this kind of versatility.

Illus. 1-1. Today's radial arm saw is superior to the original one. It is sleeker, has better guards, and has a dust-collection system.

Illus. 1-2. The radial arm saw can be used for drilling and boring. It is equipped with a work arbor. This arbor will accommodate a chuck and other accessories. A chuck is used to hold a tool in the radial arm saw.

Arbor   The metal shaft of the radial arm saw on which the circular-saw blade is mounted.

Bevel   An inclined surface that goes from face to face on stock.

Carriage   The rolling unit which is suspended from the arm of the radial arm saw.

Chamfers   Inclined surfaces that go from the face of stock to an edge.

Coarse Blade   A blade with large teeth, designed for heavy, fast, or less delicate work.

Column   The metal post which supports the arm of the radial arm saw. It is supported by the base.

Crosscut   A cut made across or against the grain of the workpiece.

Dado   A U-shaped channel made with or across the grain of the workpiece.

Dado Head   Used to cut dadoes and rabbets.

Deflection (blade)   A condition in which the circular-saw blade bounces away from or flutters in the workpiece.

Edge (of stock)   The narrower surface of a board which goes along or with the grain. The edge is usually butted to or rides along the fence.

Face (of stock)   The wider surface of a board which goes along or with the grain. One face is usually butted to or rides along the table.

Feed Speed (or rate)   The speed at which stock is fed into the radial-arm-saw blade.

Fine Blade   A blade with small teeth, designed for more delicate work.

Framing Lumber   Lumbers used for the structural member of a building, such as studs or joists.

In-Feed Side   Operator's side of the saw.

In-Ripping   A cut made with the saw's blade positioned between the fence and motor.

Jigs   Commercial or shop-made aids used to help make a cut or a series of cuts.

Kerf   The cut made by a circular-saw blade. The kerf must be larger than the saw-blade thickness.

Kickback   A condition in which a piece of stock is flung back at the operator at great speed. Usually, the stock becomes trapped between the rotating blade and a stationary object such as a fence or guard.

Lash   A condition in which a part of the radial arm saw becomes worn or loose. Lash usually occurs between two threaded parts.

Melamine   A plastic material that has been laminated to a piece of sheet stock.

Mitre Cut   An angular cut made across the face, end, or edge of the workpiece. Most mitre cuts are made at 45-degree angles, so that when the two pieces are jointed, they form a 90-degree angle.

Out-Feed Side   The side of the radial arm saw that the operator is farther from.

Out-Ripping   A cut made with the motor located between the fence and blade.

Particleboard   Sheet material made from wood chips or wood particles.

Panel Stock   Any sheet stock that is used to decorate the walls of a home.

Rabbet   An L-shaped channel that goes along the edge of a piece of stock.

Retro-Fit Accessories   Accessories that can be modified to be used with all radial arm saws.

Rip Cut   A cut made with the grain of the wood.

Sanding   Smoothing wood by grinding it with abrasives.

Sawhorse   A flat-topped trestle used singly or in pairs to support the workpiece.

Sheet Stock   Includes all wood material sold in sheets 4 feet wide and 8 to 12 feet long. Common types of sheet stock include plywood, particleboard, hardboard, and panelling.

Sliding-T-Bevel   A layout tool designed to lay out a bevel, a mitre, or an angle.

Trough   The path cut by the blade to provide clearance for the blade when ripping.

Try Square   A tool used to mark right angles on stock and also to check a corner to determine if it has been cut squarely.

True Stock   Stock with an edge and face perpendicular to each other or in a true plane.

Veneer   Thin layers bonded together to form plywood.

Vibration (Blade)   A condition in which the circular-saw blade shakes when cutting. A vibrating blade will make an uneven cut.

Yoke   The part of the carriage on a radial arm saw on which the motor is suspended.

Workpiece   The piece of wood or stock that is being cut.

Table 1-1.

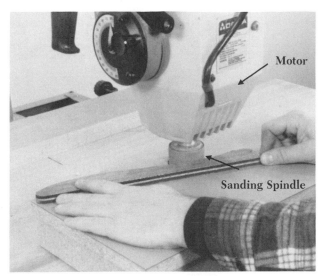

Illus. 1-3. *The radial arm saw also makes an efficient spindle sander. The work arbor drives a spindle-sanding device. Sanding techniques are examined in Chapter 5.*

Types of Cut

The radial arm saw can make eight types of cut. When the blade is in a vertical position, the saw can make a crosscut, a rip cut (in which the motor is turned 90 degrees to the work), and a mitre cut (in which the arm is turned). (See Illus. 1-4–1-6.) All these cuts are explored in Chapter 5.

Illus. 1-4. *Crosscutting is an operation in which solid wood is cut across or perpendicular to the grain.*

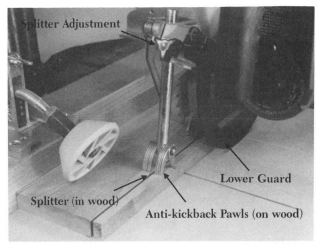

Illus. 1-5. *A rip cut is made by turning the yoke 90 degrees so that the blade is parallel to the fence. The splitter behind the blade keeps the wood from pinching the blade.*

Illus. 1-6. *A mitre cut is an angular crosscut made with the blade perpendicular to the table. Only the saw's arm is turned for this cut.*

When the blade is tilted, the radial arm saw can make a bevel (angular) crosscut (also called an end mitre), a bevel rip cut (in which the motor is turned 90 degrees to the work), and a compound mitre (in which the arm is turned). (See Illus. 1-7–1-9.) These cuts are also explored in Chapter 5.

When the blade is in the horizontal position, it can make an edge slot (also called an edge groove or edge rabbet), and an angular edge (in which the blade is tilted from the horizontal slightly).

Illus. 1-9. *A compound mitre is made when the saw's arm is turned and the blade is tilted. This cut is sometimes called a hopper cut.*

The latter cut is used chiefly for making raised panels. Before making any cuts, become familiar with the material in this chapter and the chapters that follow.

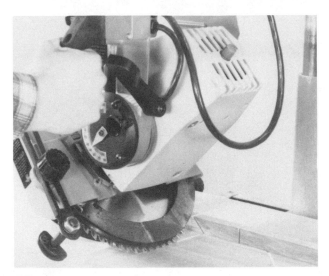

Illus. 1-7. *A bevel crosscut is a crosscut made with the blade tilted. This cut is sometimes called an end mitre. The lower blade guard acts as a barrier between the operator and the blade.*

Types of Radial Arm Saw

There are many ways of categorizing radial arm saws. The most common way is by the type of overarm they have. However, they are also categorized according to the type of yoke or drive they have. Each of these classifications is examined below.

Overarm Classifications

The radial arm saw can have a single overarm, double overarm, or retracting (gliding) overarm. The majority of machines in use today are single-overarm saws, probably because this type of saw has been on the market the longest. (See Illus. 1-10.) These radial arm saws pivot off the column at the back of the saw.

Illus. 1-8. *A bevel rip cut is made when the blade is tilted while you are making a rip cut. This cut is sometimes called an edge mitre.*

Illus. 1-10. *The single-overarm saw is the most common type of radial arm saw. This type of saw pivots off the column.*

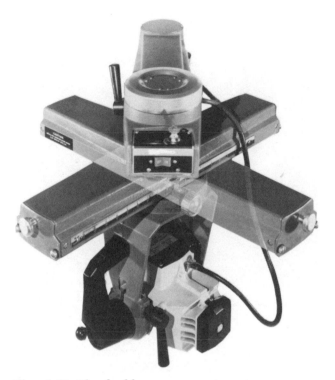

Illus. 1-12. *The double-overarm or turret-arm saw pivots from the end of the upper overarm. This allows both right and left mitres to be cut over the table. (Photo courtesy of Delta International Machinery Corp.)*

The single-overarm saw has one limitation: A long left mitre cannot be cut completely on the table. (See Illus. 1-11.) As the cut is made, the blade follows a path that leads off the table.

The double-overarm or turret-arm saw pivots from the end of the upper overarm. (See Illus. 1-12.) The lower overarm is attached to the end of the upper overarm. It is about twice as long as the upper overarm. The carriage (yoke, motor and blade unit) travels on the lower overarm. This pivoting method allows both right and left mitres to be cut over the table. (See Illus. 1-13.)

The carriage can rotate 360 degrees and the blade always cuts over the table.

The retractable- or gliding-overarm saw has an arm that glides through the column. The entire arm moves when a cut is made. The advantage with this type of radial arm saw is that the work-table is completely clear when the saw is not cutting. This leaves the table available for layout work. It also means that when you work, the saw's arm is clear of your path, which makes it possible for you to get closer to your work. The disadvantage is that the machine cannot be placed as close to the wall as other saws. There has to be clearance behind the machine for the retracting arm.

Yoke Classifications

Single- and double-overarm radial arm saws can either have a single (open) or a double (closed)

Illus. 1-11. *The single-overarm radial arm saw has one disadvantage: The blade leaves the table when a left mitre cut is made. A large auxiliary table can be used to eliminate this problem.*

Illus. 1-13. *The blade remains over the table for the entire cut on a double-overarm saw.*

yoke. A single- (open-) yoke saw has only one motor mount. (See Illus. 1-14.) The other end of the yoke is open.

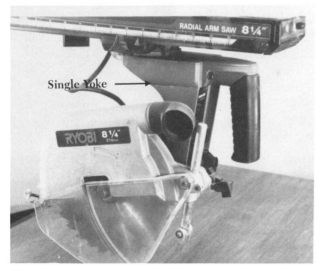

Illus. 1-14. *This single-overarm saw has a single or open yoke. The open-yoke design is not as rigid as the closed-yoke design.*

A double-yoke saw has two motor mounts, one at each end. (See Illus. 1-15.) It has a U or closed shape. The double-yoke machine provides greater vibration dampening and strength than the single-yoke machine. The double-yoke machine is much better for shaping and heavy dado work because the motor has more rigidity.

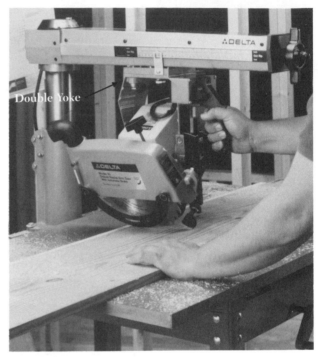

Illus. 1-15. *The closed or double-yoke radial arm saw has two motor mounts. It is much more rigid than a single-yoke saw and can be used for heavier cuts such as dadoing. (Photo courtesy of Delta International Machinery Corp.)*

Drive Classifications

Some radial arm saws have a direct-drive motor while others have a clutch-and-drive belt. A clutch-and-drive belt will slip when overloaded. This reduces the strain on the motor. The clutch will require adjustment after severe overloading of the saw. Careful operation of the saw will help you avoid adjustment problems.

A direct motor-drive saw will stall when overloaded. Most radial arm saws with a direct-drive motor have a thermal overload protector. (See Illus. 1-16.) This is a heat-actuated switch that

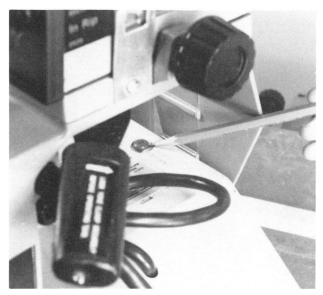

Illus. 1-16. *Direct-drive motors are protected with a thermal overload button. If the motor overheats, the thermal overload button will lift and disconnect the power of the motor. Be sure to shut off the saw before pushing the overload protector.*

opens when the motor becomes hot and disconnects the power to the motor. This protects the motor from damage.

The thermal overload protector will not close until the motor is cool enough to run safely. If the switch opens, shut the motor off and allow the motor to cool. Never attempt to hold the switch closed while turning on the saw. This is sure to damage the motor.

Determining the Size of the Radial Arm Saw

Many factors go into determining the size of a radial arm saw. Each one is important. These factors are explored below.

Blade Diameter

The most common indicator of radial-arm-saw size is blade diameter. (See Illus. 1-17.) Most radial arm saws are advertised according to the

Illus. 1-17. *The most common way of measuring radial-arm-saw size is blade diameter. The most common diameter blade used on radial arm saws is a 10-inch blade.*

largest blade that can be mounted on them. Small radial arms saws will take an 8-inch blade. The most commonly manufactured radial arm saw uses a 10-inch blade or smaller. (See Illus. 1-18.)

Blade diameter is an important indication of a radial arm saw's cutting capabilities. A 10-inch radial arm saw will cut a piece of stock 3 inches thick in half. Saws with smaller blades will not be able to cut stock as thick as 3 inches. The chart that follows gives typical cutting thicknesses; these thicknesses will vary from one brand to another. Consult the manufacturer's specifications for maximum thickness of cut.

Illus. 1-18. *Some radial arm saws use an 8- or 8½-inch-diameter blade. Even though the motor on these saws is smaller than that on saws that use larger-diameter blades, these saws can still cut stock up to 1½ inch thick at a 45-degree angle.*

Radial Arm Saw Blade Diameter		Maximum Stock-Thickness Cut	
Inches	*MM*	*Inches*	*MM*
8	203	2	51
10	254	3	76
12	305	4	102
14	356	5	127
16	406	6	152
18	457	7	178

It is possible to use a blade smaller than that specified on a radial arm saw. For example, an 8-inch blade can be used on a 10-inch radial arm saw. The smaller blade will have more power per tooth than a larger blade, but its cutting capacity will decrease.

Table Size

The size of the worktable is an important consideration when determining the size of a radial arm saw. The larger the worktable, the easier it is to handle large or heavy pieces. The typical table on a 10-inch radial arm saw is approximately 20 inches deep by 35 inches long.

Some owners add table extensions to the ends of the worktable to increase its size. These extensions may be folding or stationary extensions. (See Illus. 1-19.)

Arm Travel

Another factor that should be considered is the arm travel of the saw, which is the length of the pull stroke. The longer the pull stroke, the greater the saw's crosscutting capacity.

Arm travel is usually specified as the crosscut capacity on stock 1 inch thick. This capacity determines the maximum width of stock you can cut. Arm travel is usually greater on machines with larger-diameter blades.

Maximum Ripping Capacity

The maximum ripping capacity of the radial arm saw is an important size consideration. This capacity can affect some operations. For example, when 48-inch panels are being ripped in half, a maximum ripping capacity of 24 inches is required. (See Illus. 1-20.) Any radial arm saw that has a maximum ripping capacity of less than 24 inches would be useless if you are cutting 48-inch panels or sheet stock. Maximum ripping capacity and arm travel are usually closely related.

Horsepower

Horsepower is another very important measure of radial-arm-saw size. Almost all motors appear to be about the same size, yet some are more powerful than others. This makes motor selection confusing and difficult. The following will clarify the motor-selection process.

Rated Horsepower vs. Peak Horsepower. Horsepower is a function of torque and rpm (revolutions

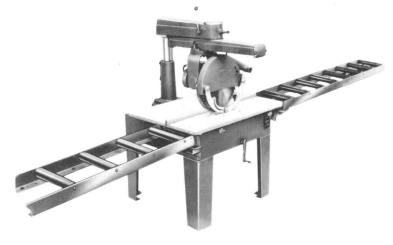

Illus. 1-19. *These stationary table extensions make it easier to control large pieces of stock. The rollers also reduce fatigue. (Photo courtesy of Delta International Machinery Corp.)*

Illus. 1-20. *To cut a sheet of plywood into two equal pieces, the radial arm saw must have a maximum ripping capacity of 24 inches. Maximum ripping capacity and arm travel are closely related. (Photo courtesy of Sears, Roebuck, & Co.)*

per minute). The peak or developed horsepower of the motor is the horsepower of the motor when its only load is the saw blade. Rated horsepower is the horsepower of the motor under load. Rated horsepower is lower than peak horsepower.

Generally, the best comparison between motors is the amperage rating. A 10-ampere, 110-volt motor has an actual horsepower of about one.

Under actual working conditions, the electrical supply can affect horsepower and radial-arm-saw effectiveness. There must be adequate voltage and amperage for the motor to gain total horsepower. A 15-ampere circuit is the absolute minimum that should be used with a radial arm saw. If an extension cord is used to connect the saw to the circuit, make sure that the cord can handle the load without a large drop in amperage or voltage. Use an extension cord with a number 10 or 12 wire gauge. Consult your operator's manual for specifics.

How Much Horsepower Is Needed? The motors on most radial arm saws range in horsepower from 1 horsepower (rated) to 7 horsepower (rated). This is a considerable difference in horsepower. A 1-horsepower motor would be found on an 8- or 10-inch saw. This is because the saw turns a smaller blade and is not designed to cut thick stock. A 12- or 16-inch radial arm saw would have a 5- to 7-horsepower (rated) motor. A 10-inch radial arm saw could have a 1-, 1½-, 2- or 3-horsepower motor (rated).

The large variation in horsepower is due to the different jobs these saws might perform. If a 10-inch radial arm saw were used to cut framing lumber, a 2- or 3-horsepower (rated) motor would be selected. This is because framing lumber has a higher moisture content and is not as true as furniture lumber. Increased moisture in wood requires a saw with more horsepower so that it can throw or eject the heavier sawdust.

Radial arm saws that are purchased for heavy ripping or dadoing operations should be equipped with the largest available horsepower motor. Ripping requires about five times as much energy as crosscutting. Turning a large dado head and making dado cuts require much more power than general ripping or crosscutting. (Ripping, dadoing, and crosscutting are examined in Chapter 5.)

In most cases, a 10-inch radial arm saw is underpowered if it has a 1-horsepower (rated) or smaller motor. A 12-ampere, or about 1.5-horsepower (rated), motor should be the smallest one used on a 10-inch radial arm saw intended for general service. A 10-inch radial arm saw with an 8-inch-diameter blade mounted on the arbor will have more cutting power because less power is needed to turn the smaller blade. When using a smaller blade, make sure that the arbor hole and rpm rating are correct for your saw.

Larger-horsepower motors can do a larger job, but because they have more power they have more of a capacity for kickback (ejecting stock towards you). Stock that binds on a lower-horsepower radial arm saw is likely to freeze the blade rather than kick back.

When selecting a radial arm saw, determine the proper horsepower according to the work you do. Evaluate all available radial arm saws carefully before selecting one.

What Voltage Is Desirable? Most 10-inch radial arm saws draw 15 amperes or less. This is considered appropriate for 110-volt household circuits.

Some saws can be modified to run on 220-volt household circuits. There will be more power and less strain on the electrical system when the saw runs at 220 volts.

Most 12-inch radial arm saws require 220 volts because they draw 18 to 20 amperes. This may be too much of a strain for the typical 110-volt household system.

The outlets for 110 volts and 220 volts differ in configuration. This eliminates the chance of using too much or too little voltage. Make sure that the plug and outlet are appropriate for your saw.

Controls

There are five common controls on the radial arm saw: the power switch, the elevating crank, the arm, the motor, and the yoke. (See Illus. 1-21–1-23.) In some cases, radial arm saws have a brake. This may be an electronic control related to the switch, or it may be mechanical.

Note: Whenever adjusting blade elevation, blade angle, arm angle, or yoke position, always make a cut in the table and a cut in the fence at the same time. Before cutting into the table or

Illus. 1-21. *Study the parts and controls on this radial arm saw. Compare the controls to those on your saw and those in Illus. 1-22 and 1-23.*

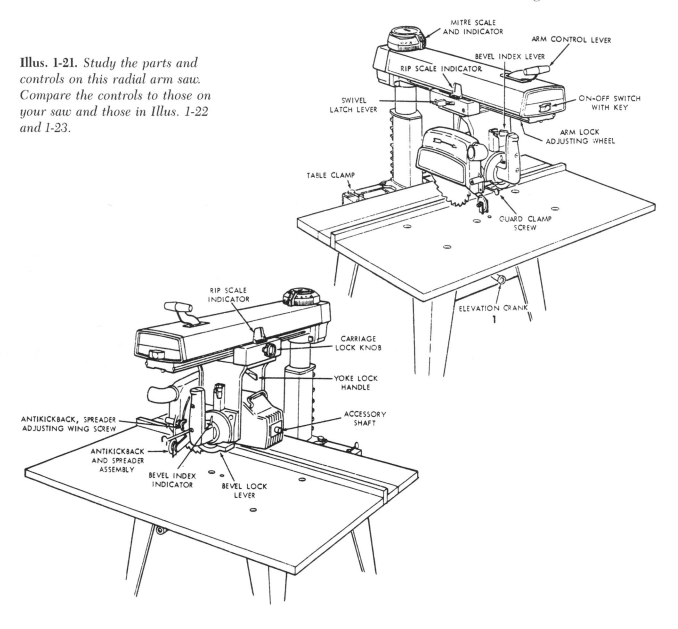

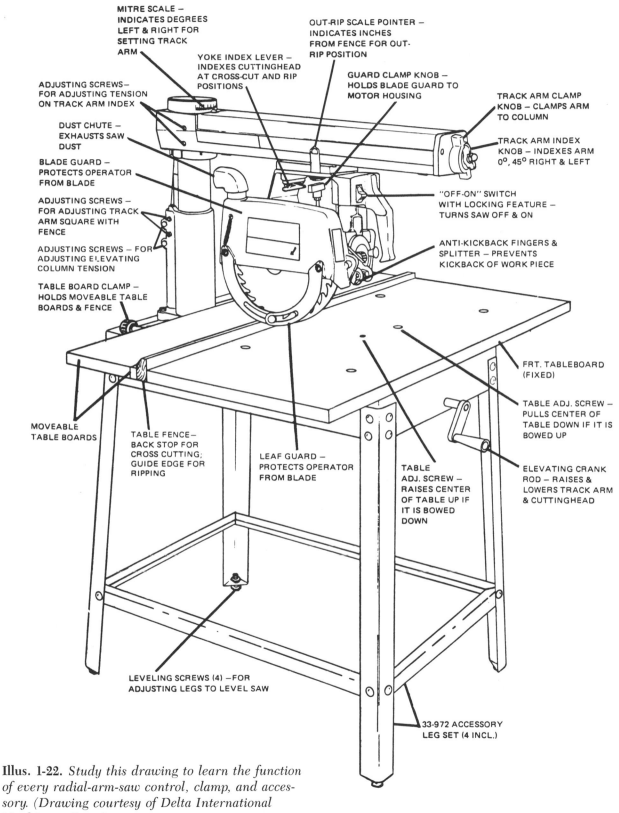

MITRE SCALE – INDICATES DEGREES LEFT & RIGHT FOR SETTING TRACK ARM

OUT-RIP SCALE POINTER – INDICATES INCHES FROM FENCE FOR OUT-RIP POSITION

YOKE INDEX LEVER – INDEXES CUTTINGHEAD AT CROSS-CUT AND RIP POSITIONS

GUARD CLAMP KNOB – HOLDS BLADE GUARD TO MOTOR HOUSING

ADJUSTING SCREWS– FOR ADJUSTING TENSION ON TRACK ARM INDEX

TRACK ARM CLAMP KNOB – CLAMPS ARM TO COLUMN

DUST CHUTE – EXHAUSTS SAW DUST

TRACK ARM INDEX KNOB – INDEXES ARM 0º, 45º RIGHT & LEFT

BLADE GUARD – PROTECTS OPERATOR FROM BLADE

"OFF-ON" SWITCH WITH LOCKING FEATURE – TURNS SAW OFF & ON

ADJUSTING SCREWS – FOR ADJUSTING TRACK ARM SQUARE WITH FENCE

ADJUSTING SCREWS – FOR ADJUSTING ELEVATING COLUMN TENSION

ANTI-KICKBACK FINGERS & SPLITTER – PREVENTS KICKBACK OF WORK PIECE

TABLE BOARD CLAMP – HOLDS MOVEABLE TABLE BOARDS & FENCE

FRT. TABLEBOARD (FIXED)

MOVEABLE TABLE BOARDS

TABLE FENCE– BACK STOP FOR CROSS CUTTING; GUIDE EDGE FOR RIPPING

LEAF GUARD – PROTECTS OPERATOR FROM BLADE

TABLE ADJ. SCREW – RAISES CENTER OF TABLE UP IF IT IS BOWED DOWN

TABLE ADJ. SCREW – PULLS CENTER OF TABLE DOWN IF IT IS BOWED UP

ELEVATING CRANK ROD – RAISES & LOWERS TRACK ARM & CUTTINGHEAD

LEVELING SCREWS (4) –FOR ADJUSTING LEGS TO LEVEL SAW

33-972 ACCESSORY LEG SET (4 INCL.)

Illus. 1-22. *Study this drawing to learn the function of every radial-arm-saw control, clamp, and accessory. (Drawing courtesy of Delta International Machinery Corp.)*

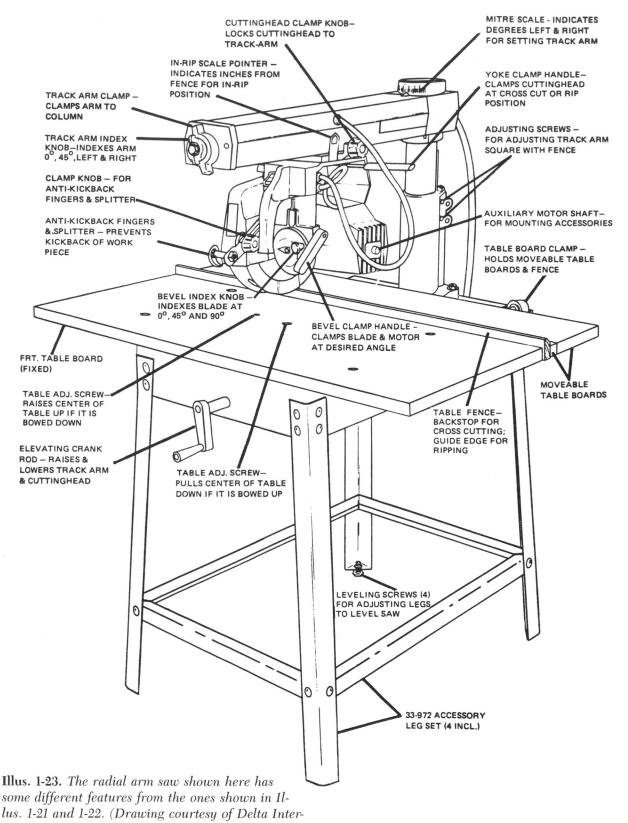

CUTTINGHEAD CLAMP KNOB—
LOCKS CUTTINGHEAD TO
TRACK-ARM

MITRE SCALE - INDICATES
DEGREES LEFT & RIGHT
FOR SETTING TRACK ARM

IN-RIP SCALE POINTER —
INDICATES INCHES FROM
FENCE FOR IN-RIP
POSITION

YOKE CLAMP HANDLE—
CLAMPS CUTTINGHEAD
AT CROSS CUT OR RIP
POSITION

TRACK ARM CLAMP —
CLAMPS ARM TO
COLUMN

ADJUSTING SCREWS —
FOR ADJUSTING TRACK ARM
SQUARE WITH FENCE

TRACK ARM INDEX
KNOB—INDEXES ARM
0°, 45°, LEFT & RIGHT

CLAMP KNOB — FOR
ANTI-KICKBACK
FINGERS & SPLITTER

AUXILIARY MOTOR SHAFT—
FOR MOUNTING ACCESSORIES

ANTI-KICKBACK FINGERS
&.SPLITTER — PREVENTS
KICKBACK OF WORK
PIECE

TABLE BOARD CLAMP —
HOLDS MOVEABLE TABLE
BOARDS & FENCE

BEVEL INDEX KNOB —
INDEXES BLADE AT
0°, 45° AND 90°

BEVEL CLAMP HANDLE -
CLAMPS BLADE & MOTOR
AT DESIRED ANGLE

FRT. TABLE BOARD
(FIXED)

MOVEABLE
TABLE BOARDS

TABLE ADJ. SCREW—
RAISES CENTER OF
TABLE UP IF IT IS
BOWED DOWN

TABLE FENCE—
BACKSTOP FOR
CROSS CUTTING;
GUIDE EDGE FOR
RIPPING

ELEVATING CRANK
ROD — RAISES &
LOWERS TRACK ARM
& CUTTINGHEAD

TABLE ADJ. SCREW—
PULLS CENTER OF TABLE
DOWN IF IT IS BOWED UP

LEVELING SCREWS (4)
FOR ADJUSTING LEGS
TO LEVEL SAW

33-972 ACCESSORY
LEG SET (4 INCL.)

Illus. 1-23. *The radial arm saw shown here has some different features from the ones shown in Illus. 1-21 and 1-22. (Drawing courtesy of Delta International Machinery Corp.)*

fence, make sure that the blade will only contact wood. Check for metal table clamps or table fasteners that may be in the blade's path. (See Illus. 1-24.) Contact with metal parts dulls or damages the blade and may cause injury due to flying metal parts.

Each of the five common controls is examined below.

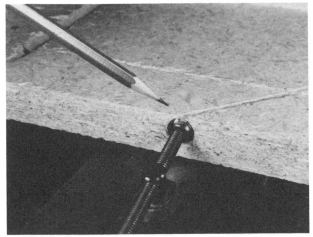

Illus. 1-24. *Check the blade's path before turning on the radial arm saw. The blade actually cut into this table clamp. An auxiliary front table would have eliminated contact between the blade and table clamp.*

Power Switch

There are many different types of power switch used on radial arm saws. (See Illus. 1-25.) Some are push-button switches, and others are flip-type switches. For safety purposes, some of these switches are designed so that they are easier to turn off than on. When color-coding is used, red is used to designate "off" and green "on." (See Illus. 1-26.)

The power switch is positioned so that the saw can be turned on and off easily without reaching. Some saws have the switch on the end of the arm. On other saws, the switch is located close to the pull handle on the yoke. (See Illus. 1-27.) This type of switch is handier for crosscutting, but when the yoke is turned for ripping, the switch is on the other side of the machine. This makes it difficult to turn off the saw in an emergency. The switch on some saws is located under the table.

Newer machines have a better switch that is positioned for safety. The switch on old radial arm saws is located at the back of the machine on the column. These switches are difficult to reach in an emergency.

On some power switches, a key has to be inserted before the radial arm saw can be used. (See

Illus. 1-25. *This rocker switch is located on the upper overarm of the radial arm saw. It is convenient for rip cuts or crosscuts. Note the locking mechanism. The saw cannot be started if it is locked.*

Illus. 1-26. *The power switch on the end of the radial arm saw is color-coded. Red is off, and green is on. The rod to the right of the switch can be removed to prevent start-up by unauthorized persons.*

Illus. 1-27. *The flip switch on this radial arm saw is located on the yoke. This position is more convenient for crosscutting than ripping. The center of this switch can be removed to prevent start-up by unauthorized persons.*

Illus. 1-28.) This type of switch keeps inexperienced operators and curious children from operating the saw. Key-actuated switches should always be used on tools in a home where children live or visit.

On high-voltage radial arm saws, a low-voltage switching system is used. The system uses a 24-volt circuit to the motor. This system activates a solenoid on the motor to the on or off position. The 24-volt circuit minimizes the chance of high-voltage electric shock to the operator.

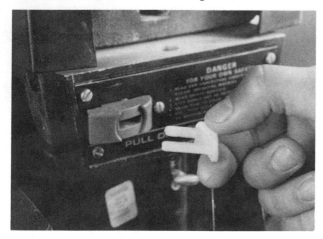

Illus. 1-28. *This key is actually part of the switch. When it is removed, the saw cannot be started. Be sure to keep the key in a secure place.*

Crank

Blade elevation is controlled by a crank. This crank may be on top of the column or arm, or it may be under the table at the front of the saw. (See Illus. 1-29 and 1-30.) Most cranks have an arrow to indicate turning directions for raising the blade.

Learn how much one turn of the elevating crank raises or lowers the blade. This knowledge will be valuable to you when making minor blade-height adjustments. For instance, if one revolution of the crank raises (or lowers) the blade ⅛ inch, then ½ revolution of the elevating crank would raise (or lower) the blade ⅟16 inch. If you understand the relationship between blade height and the elevating crank, it will be easier and faster to set up the saw.

Some older machines have lash (slop or looseness) in the elevating mechanism. In such cases, it may mean that the blade elevation will change as the operation progresses. If lash exists on your radial arm saw, make the final blade-height adjustment by raising the blade. This will ensure positive gear engagement and prevent elevation change during the operation.

Illus. 1-29. *The blade-elevating crank on this radial arm saw is located on the column. This type of elevating system is less likely to have gear lash problems (looseness in the elevating mechanism).*

Illus. 1-30. *The blade-elevating crank on this radial arm saw is located at the front of the saw under the table. A blade-elevating crank in such a location can be reached more conveniently.*

Arm

The arm on a radial arm saw is turned so that the radial arm saw can make angular cuts such as mitres. Arm-turning is also known as radial arm swing or pivot. The arm is usually locked and clamped in the 0 position on the elevating mechanism. This is the position used for crosscutting. (See Illus. 1-31.) The arm can also be locked and clamped at angles such as 45 degrees left or right. When other angles are cut, the lock does

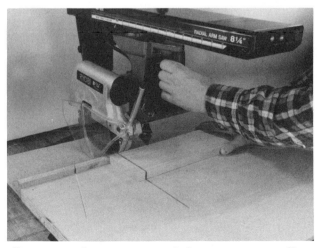

Illus. 1-31. *The arm on a radial arm saw is usually locked in the 0 position for crosscutting. The arm can be turned to make mitre cuts.*

not engage, but holds the arm securely at the desired angle.

To pivot the radial arm, loosen the locking device and release the clamp. The lock and clamp are located at the front of the arm on some radial arm saws, and at the top of the column on others. (See Illus. 1-32.) On turret-arm saws, the lock

Illus. 1-32. *This lock provides positive stopping between the arm and column. Note the blade-elevating handwheel on top of the column.*

and clamp are found at the junction of the upper and lower arms.

Make sure that the blade is elevated above the fence and table before pivoting the arm. (See Illus. 1-33.) If the blade is not raised, damage could occur to the blade, fence, or table. Set the desired angle using the indicator on top of the column. Engage the lock (if possible) and secure the clamp.

Now, cut a kerf into the fence and table. (Fences are examined under the heading "Accessories" later in this chapter.) Push the motor unit all the way back against the column and turn on the saw. With one hand on the handle, slowly lower the blade until it touches the table. Slowly pull the motor through the length of its stroke to cut a kerf. Return the motor to the column and repeat the process until the kerf in the table is ¹⁄₁₆–¹⁄₈ inch deep. (See Illus. 1-34.) Avoid making any table kerf too deep. It could interfere with rip cuts.

Motor

To tilt the blade, pivot the motor in the yoke. (See Illus. 1-35.) The blade is tilted to cut bevels,

Illus. 1-33. *The lock on this saw is located on the end of the arm. Make sure that the blade is raised above the table before turning the arm.*

Lock

Illus. 1-34. *Cut a kerf on the fence. The kerf should be no more than ⅛ inch deep. Pull the carriage slowly towards you. Make sure that there are no metal parts in the blade's path.*

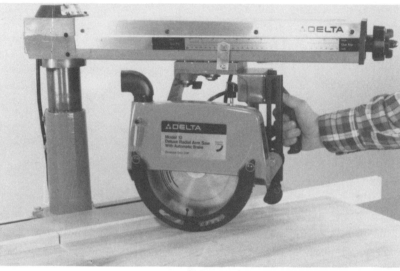

Illus. 1-35. *Pivot the motor in the yoke to make bevel or end-mitre cuts. Make sure that all clamps are locked securely before making any cuts.*

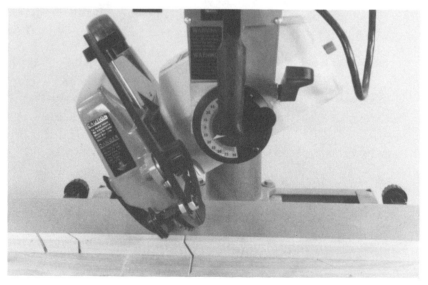

chamfers, and end mitres. (These types of cut are examined in Chapter 5.) When the blade is tilted and the arm is turned, the radial arm saw can make compound mitres or hopper cuts. (See Illus. 1-36.) The blade is also tilted when devices

Illus. 1-36. *When the arm is turned and the motor is pivoted, a compound mitre, or hopper, cut is made. Make sure that all clamps are locked securely before making any cuts.*

such as sanding discs are used to sand bevels or chamfers.

The motor is held in the 0 position (perpendicular to the table) with a lock and clamp. The lock and clamp also hold the blade in position at angles of 45 and 90 degrees (horizontal or parallel to the table). When other blade angles are set, the clamp holds the blade (and motor) at the desired angle.

To tilt or turn the blade, disconnect the power and raise the blade above the table while it is back at the column. (See Illus. 1-37.) To do this, loosen the clamp and place your hand on the handle. Release the lock pin. (See Illus. 1-38.) Then twist the handle to tilt the blade. (See Illus. 1-39.) The indicator on the yoke will tell you when the desired angle has been reached. (See Illus. 1-40.) With some angles, the lock will fall into place. Other angles can only be held with a clamp. Tighten the clamp securely.

Now, cut a kerf into the fence and table. Turn on the saw with the motor located all the way

back at the column. With one hand on the handle, slowly lower the blade until it touches the table. Pull the motor through the length of its stroke. (See Illus. 1-41.) This will cut a kerf through the fence and into the table. Return the motor to the column and repeat if necessary. The kerf in the table should be about 1/16 to 1/8 inch deep.

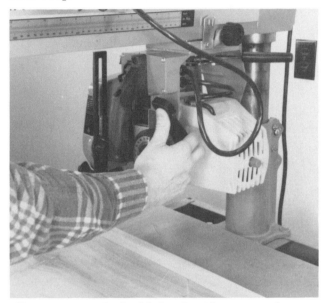

Illus. 1-37. *To tilt the blade, first disconnect the power and then release the clamp. Make sure that the blade will clear the table.*

Illus. 1-38. *Release the lock pin, which holds the motor perpendicular to the table. It may be necessary to support the motor while doing this.*

Illus. 1-39. *Turn the motor to the desired angle and tighten the clamp. The lock pin will engage at 45 degrees only.*

Illus. 1-40. *Use the protractor scale as an indicator of blade angle.*

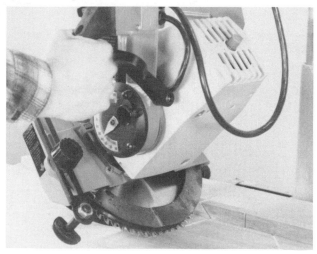

Motor and Yoke

The motor and yoke are pivoted mostly for ripping operations. (See Illus. 1-42 and 1-43.) The yoke is pivoted so that the blade is parallel to the fence. The motor and blade are attached to the yoke, and pivot together. When the blade is between the fence and motor, the cutting process is known as in-ripping. (See Illus. 1-44.) When the motor is between the fence and blade, it is known as out-ripping. (See Illus. 1-45.) The motor and yoke are also pivoted for other operations such as sanding.

To pivot the yoke, pull the yoke and carriage (the unit that holds the yoke to the arm) to the middle of its stroke and lock the carriage. Release the yoke clamp, which is located between the motor and carriage. Lift the yoke-locking pin and turn the yoke to its desired position. Now, cut a rip trough. (See Illus. 1-46.) To do this, turn on the motor and lower the blade until it touches the table. (See Illus. 1-47.) Grasp the handle securely and release the carriage lock. Move the carriage slowly throughout its stroke, being careful not to hit the fence. Lower the blade and repeat the process until the trough is 1/16–1/8 inch deep. (See Illus. 1-48.) Now, move the blade in the trough to adjust for any change in the width of the rip cut.

If you wish to make a rip cut in the stock at an angle, tilt the blade to the desired angle after the rip trough has been cut. (See Illus. 1-49.) You may have to readjust the blade height. Make this adjustment carefully so that the blade does not hit the table and become damaged.

Brake

Some radial arm saws made today are equipped with an electronic brake. This brake stops the blade by sending a current through the motor.

Illus. 1-41 (left). *Cut a kerf on the fence and table at the desired angle. Do not cut too deeply into the table.*

Illus. 1-42. *The motor and yoke have been pivoted for a ripping operation. The Shophelper hold-down and anti-kickback pawls make the operation safer. (See the Accessories section on pages 25–38 for information on Shophelper hold-downs and pawls.)*

Illus. 1-43. *The yoke pivots at the underside of the carriage. The carriage rides on the arm.*

Illus. 1-44. *When the blade is between the fence and motor, the cutting process is known as in-ripping. This is the favored position for right-handers.*

Illus. 1-45. *When the motor is between the fence and the blade, the cutting process is known as outripping. This position is favored for making wide rip cuts in sheet stock.*

Illus. 1-46. *The rip trough cut into the table allows a rip cut of any width to be set easily. More information on ripping can be found in Chapter 5.*

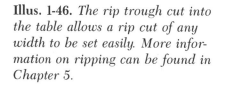

Illus. 1-47. *Turn on the saw and lower the blade until it cuts the table lightly. Pull the carriage through its stroke.*

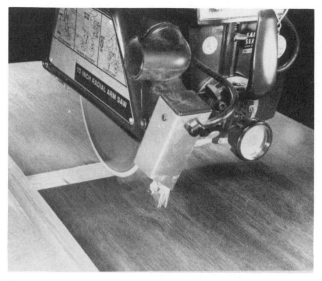

Illus. 1-48. *Lower the blade again so that the trough can be cut to a depth of ¹⁄₁₆ inch.*

Illus. 1-49. *If you want to make a rip cut at an angle (bevel-rip), tilt the blade to the desired angle after cutting the rip trough.*

The current counteracts the motion of the motor, causing it to stop. An electronic brake can be retrofitted to most radial arm saws. (A retrofitted part is a part that did not originally come with the tool, but can be added to the tool.) For additional information, consult an industrial woodworking machinery catalogue or agent.

The brake makes the radial arm saw safer to operate. The operator does not have to wait for the motor to coast to a stop before changing the setup. The electronic brake causes no appreciable wear on the motor.

Note: When the radial arm saw is equipped with an electronic brake, make sure that the arbor nut that holds the blade in position is tightened securely. The sudden stop caused by the brake can cause the nut and blade to loosen. Check the arbor nut for tightness periodically. Rapidly cycling a saw on and off when it is equipped with a brake can loosen the nut and blade.

Other radial arm saws have a mechanical brake. This brake goes over the auxiliary arbor. The auxiliary arbor is located on the motor opposite the saw arbor. The mechanical brake is depressed after the saw has been shut off. Mechanical brakes are likely to be found on older radial arm saws. Newer saws will have an electronic brake.

Accessories

There are numerous accessories available for the radial arm saw. These accessories make the radial arm saw more versatile, safer, and easier to use. Some accessories may come with the saw or may be sold as extras or options. Others are designed and made in the shop for a specific purpose.

Power Takeoff Shafts

Many radial arm saws have a power takeoff shaft on the end of the motor opposite the blade arbor. (See Illus. 1-50.) This shaft is designed to accommodate work accessories such as a drill chuck or router collet. There are many work accessories available for the radial arm saw.

The power takeoff shaft is usually threaded. Accessories are mounted on the threaded shaft. When the shaft is not in use, a plastic cap can be attached to it. This cap protects the threads from damage.

On some radial arm saws, the power takeoff shaft doubles as a brake. When the power takeoff shaft is needed, the brake is removed and the braking wheel is unscrewed from the threaded shaft. The speed at which this shaft turns may be different from that of the saw arbor. Some arbors are designed to be used as a router. They turn at speeds far too great for anything but a router bit. Make sure that they are used only for router bits. (See Illus. 1-51.)

Illus. 1-50. The power takeoff shaft or work arbor is designed to accommodate work accessories such as a router collet or drill chuck.

Illus. 1-51. This power takeoff shaft is designed for router bits. It turns about four times as fast as the blade arbor. This power takeoff can only be used for router bits.

Table Boards and Fences

Most radial arms saws have three table boards, the largest of which is fastened to the saw frame. The two smaller boards and fences are held in position with table clamps. (See Illus. 1-52.) These clamps can be actuated at the front or back of the saw. (See Illus. 1-53.) The fence is located between the table boards. The clamps hold it in position also. The three table boards are called the front table, the rear table, and the spacer board. The front table is the widest table board. The rear table is narrower than the front table. The spacer board is the narrowest piece.

There are three possible fence positions, as shown in Illus. 1-54: 1, the typical or usual position; 2, the position for crosscutting wide pieces of 1-inch-thick stock or for increased mitre and bevel capability; and 3, the position for the widest possible rip cut (in the out-rip position.) (See Illus. 1-55.)

Most table boards are made of ¾- or 1-inch-thick particle board or plywood. Particleboard holds up better. When the tables have been cut up many times for different operations, they are replaced. Holes are sometimes cut in the rear table to accommodate a spindle sander.

Some woodworkers screw, nail, or clamp an auxiliary front table on top of the front table. (See Illus. 1-56.) This table should be from ¼ to ¾ inch thick.

The auxiliary table is easier to replace and keeps the front table in good shape. It also elevates the work, which is necessary when working with the blade in the horizontal position.

The fence supplied with the radial arm saw is usually made of ¾- or 1-inch-thick particleboard. It is approximately 2 inches wide and about the length of the front and rear tables. The fence is replaced frequently, because the kerfs made for different operations weaken it or cause projections that affect accuracy.

Most woodworkers make replacement fences in different sizes and shaped for special setups and jobs. Some fences are made for a specific job, and are only installed for that job. They are removed immediately after the job is completed.

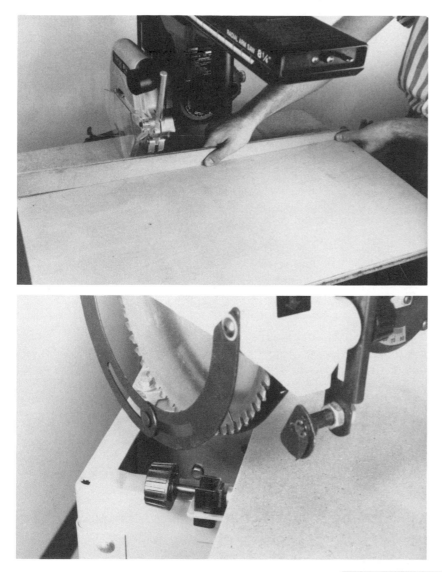

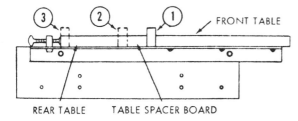

Illus. 1-52. *The smaller boards and fence are held in position by the table clamps.*

Illus. 1-53. *These clamps are actuated from the rear of the table. Some table clamps are actuated from the front of the saw.*

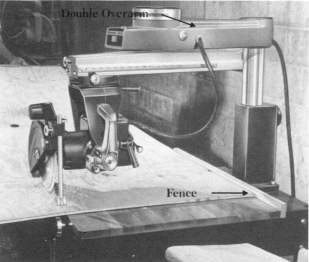

Illus. 1-54 (above). *Note the three possible fence positions. Consult the text for the use of each position. (Drawing courtesy of Sears, Roebuck, & Co.)* **Illus. 1-55 (right).** *The fence on this radial arm saw is in position three. The saw is set up for out-ripping. This allows the operator to make the widest possible rip cut.*

Illus. 1-56. *Some woodworkers attach a wooden auxiliary table over the existing table. This table can be nailed or screwed to the original table. Make sure that the nails or screws are not in the blade's path.*

Thick fences may require that a different-size spacer board be used. This is because the table clamps cannot be adjusted enough to accommodate the thicker fence.

The fences shown throughout this book are of different thicknesses, widths, lengths, and shapes. They were made in the shop specifically for the job at hand. Make up some extra fences as one of your first radial-arm-saw projects. That way, they will be ready when you wish to try some advanced setups. Make the fences out of particleboard, plywood, or solid stock. The fence must be true, smooth, and rigid enough for the operation being performed.

See Chapter 7 to learn how to make certain fences.

Blade Dampeners and Collars

Blade dampeners and collars are used adjacent to the blade. They improve the quality of the saw cut and reduce noise and blade wear.

A dampener is a flat disc of steel that goes next to the blade usually closest to the arbor nut. (See Illus. 1-57.) The dampener does as its name implies: It dampens vibration. This occurs in the same way vibration is dampened when you silence a ringing bell by placing a hand on it. The

Saw-Blade Dampener

Illus. 1-57. *A saw-blade dampener reduces vibrations and noise. The dampener also improves the cut and reduces blade wear. Mount the dampener to the blade closest to the arbor nut. This will keep the blade aligned with the splitter.*

reduction in vibration reduces noise, improves the quality of the cut, and reduces wear on the blade. Blade wear is reduced because the blade travels in a straighter line.

Blade collars are used in pairs. (See Illus. 1-58.) The collars are hollow-ground; the hollow-ground sides face the blade. The blade is then

Illus. 1-58. *Blade collars are used in pairs. Make sure that the hollow-ground sides of the collar face the blade. Blade collars help hold the blade in a true orbit by resisting deflection. Be sure to realign the splitter with the blade.*

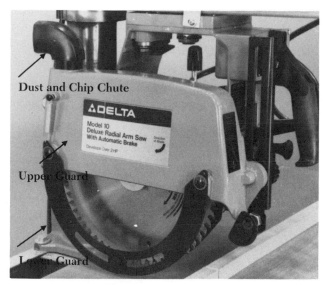

Illus. 1-59. *The upper and lower guards act as a barrier between the operator and the blade.*

clamped into a truer orbit. This causes the blade to run smoother and with less deflection. Saw-blade collars are also known as stabilizers.

When using either collars or a dampener, be sure that the splitter is aligned with the blade.

Guards

There are two common guards used on the radial arm saw: the upper guard and the lower guard. The upper and lower guards are used for most common radial-arm-saw operations. (See Illus. 1-59.)

The purpose of these guards is to protect the operator from contact with the blade. Most radial-arm-saw guards attach to the motor housing. They are easy to remove, so setup and blade changes can be done easily.

Lower-guard contact with the blade is not un-common. Movement of the stock under the lower guard can sometimes push the lower guard against the blade's teeth. The lower guard is

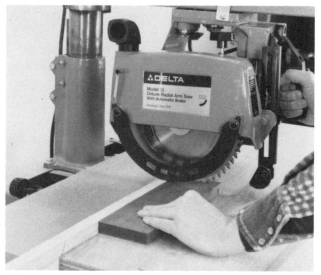

Illus. 1-60. *The lower guard is lifted over the work-piece when a cut is made.*

lifted over the work as the cut is made. (See Illus. 1-60.)

The upper guard does not contact the blade if it is installed properly and the correct blade has been mounted on the arbor. When in doubt, turn the blade over by hand to make certain it does not touch the guard. *Do this with the power disconnected.*

Splitter

The splitter and anti-kickback pawls are suspended from the upper guard. (See Illus. 1-61.) They adjust up and down, and are locked in place by a thumbscrew or wing nut. The splitter and anti-kickback pawls are used only for rip cuts. They are raised out of the way for cross-cutting.

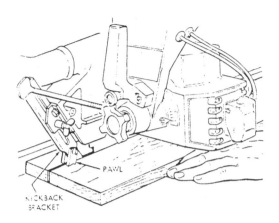

Illus. 1-62. *The anti-kickback pawls ride on the work. If the work begins to kick back, the pawls dig into it. The pawls must be kept sharp to be effective. (Drawing courtesy of Sears, Roebuck, & Co.)*

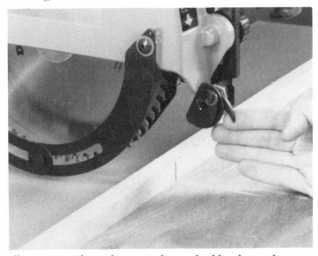

Illus. 1-61. *The splitter and anti-kickback pawls are suspended from the upper guard. The splitter keeps the saw kerf open during a rip cut. The anti-kickback pawls ride on the work and guard against kickback.*

The splitter rides in the saw kerf and holds the kerf open as the stock is being cut. This minimizes the chances of the stock pinching the blade and causing a kickback. A kickback occurs when the stock is thrown towards the operator with great speed, possibly causing injury.

The anti-kickback pawls ride on the stock while it is being cut. They are very sharp. If the stock begins to kick back, the pawls dig into the wood and stop the kickback. The pawls must be kept sharp and positioned correctly to be effective. (See Illus. 1-62.)

The splitter and anti-kickback pawls can be an effective guard when you are crosscutting, too. Some woodworkers make the mistake of positioning their hands in the blade's path. When the splitter and anti-kickback pawls just clear the wood, they act as a barrier and will knock the

Illus. 1-63. *When the splitter and anti-kickback pawls just clear the wood, they can act as a barrier and will knock the operator's hand out of the blade's path.*

operator's hand out of the blade's path. (See Illus. 1-63.) This can prevent an accident.

The splitter can become loose during an operation. It can actually drop into the saw blade and damage the blade (and anti-kickback pawls). (See Illus. 1-68.) Always check the splitter to be sure that it is locked securely in position.

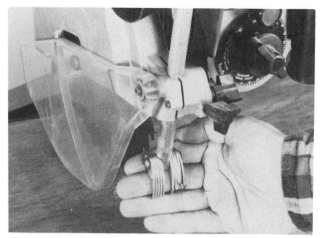

Illus. 1-64. *The splitter can become loose during an operation. This one dropped into the blade. The blade and splitter were both damaged. Check the splitter periodically to be sure that it is clamped securely.*

Return Spring

The return spring is an accessory that pulls the carriage back to the column. (See Illus. 1-65.) When the carriage is released during a pull stroke, this spring-loaded accessory returns it to its resting position. The Occupational Safety and Health Administration (OSHA) has written legislation concerning this aspect of the radial arm saw. One of its guidelines is as follows: "Installation shall be in such a manner that the front end of the unit will be slightly higher than the rear, so as to cause the cutting head to return gently to the starting position when released by the opera-tor." The return spring complies with the OSHA regulations concerning industrial use and makes the saw safer in a home or small shop operation. Some springs simply hook over the carriage lock knob.

Arm Clamp

The arm clamp (sometimes called an arm stop, carriage stop, or carriage clamp) locks to the arm of the radial arm saw. (See Illus. 1-66.) The arm clamp limits the movement of the carriage. This makes repetitive cuts safer. You cannot pull the blade beyond the work. Arm clamps can also be used for blind dadoes. When the carriage hits the clamp, blade travel stops.

Arm clamps are required by OSHA on saws doing repetitive work. Another OSHA guideline states: "An adjustable stop shall be provided to prevent the forward travel of the blade beyond the position necessary to complete the cut in repetitive operation."

When arm clamps are not available for a particular saw, they can be made from wood, or a piece of scrap can be clamped to the arm. (See Illus. 1-67.)

Featherboard

A featherboard is a shop-made device used to help control stock. (See Illus. 1-68.) It is a piece

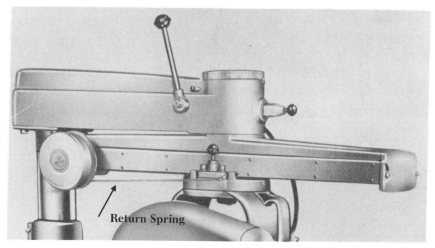

Return Spring

Illus. **1-65.** *Some return springs simply hook over the lock knob or clamp onto the carriage. These types of spring can be easily removed for specialty setups. (Photo courtesy of Delta International Machinery Corp.)*

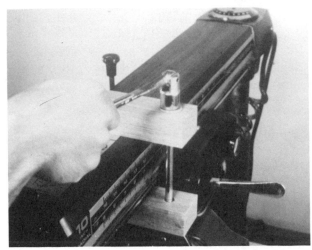

Illus. 1-66. *The arm clamp locks to the arm of the radial arm saw. It limits the stroke of the carriage during repetitive cuts.*

Illus. 1-67. *You can also make your own arm clamp. Tighten the clamp securely before starting the saw.*

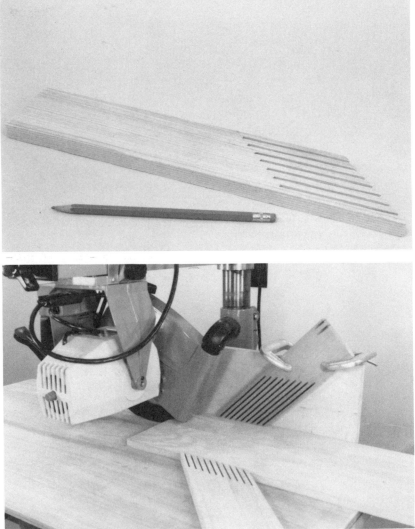

Illus. 1-68. *The featherboard is a shop-made device used to help control stock.*

Illus. 1-69. *Featherboards can be clamped to the table or fence to control stock.*

of solid stock with several kerfs spaced along or with the grain. The end of the piece is cut at a 30-45-degree angle.

The featherboard (referred to as a comb in OSHA regulations) is clamped to the table or fence. (See Illus. 1-69.) It holds stock against the fence or table. The featherboard acts like a spring. The feathers force stock against the fence or table. They help minimize kickback hazards and reduce vibration. Vibration is a chief cause of blade dulling.

Chapter 7 contains instructions for making a featherboard.

Commercial Hold-downs

Commercial hold-downs are devices designed to do the job of a featherboard. They hold stock down on the table and against the fence. Commercial hold-downs are much better to use than shop-made featherboards.

There are three commercial hold-downs on the market today: spring-steel hold-downs, Ripstrate® hold-downs, and Shophelper® hold-downs.

Spring-steel hold-downs can be used to feed from either end of the fence. Four spring-steel pieces on the hold-down hold the work in position. (See Illus. 1-70.) The position of the springs is adjusted relative to the work. Note that the out-feed side of the hold-down (the side away from the operator) must be adjusted correctly or the work will not lift the springs, which are held

in position with a setscrew. A shaper fence design accompanies a set of spring-steel hold-downs.

The Ripstrate hold-down is designed to hold the stock down on the table and against the fence during rip cuts. (See Illus. 1-71.) The Ripstrate also acts as an anti-kickback device. If the work begins to kick back, the wheels lock and resist it.

The Ripstrate can be completely reversed, so you can use it to feed stock from either side of the saw. To do this, you have to make a special fence and clamp the Ripstrate hold-down to it.

Shophelper hold-downs are used to hold stock against the table and fence, reduce vibration, and reduce the chance of a kickback. The large, plastic wheels on the hold-down hold the work down on the table and in against the fence. They slide in and out of metal brackets that are screwed to an auxiliary fence. (See Illus. 1-72.) These wheels turn in only one direction, so they act as an anti-kickback device. Since they turn in only one direction, one pair (colored yellow) is needed for in-ripping, and one pair (colored orange) is needed for out-ripping.

You can adjust the tension of the wheels on a Shophelper hold-down by moving them and turning the wing nut on the end of the spring. The wheels can also be moved to any position on the work.

Table Clamp

The table clamp is a hold-down used on the radial arm saw for crosscutting operations. The

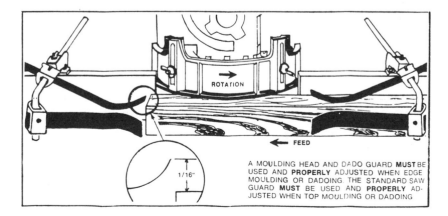

A MOULDING HEAD AND DADO GUARD **MUST** BE USED AND **PROPERLY** ADJUSTED WHEN EDGE MOULDING OR DADOING. THE STANDARD SAW GUARD **MUST** BE USED AND **PROPERLY** ADJUSTED WHEN TOP MOULDING OR DADOING

Illus. 1-70. This commercial hold-down uses spring steel to hold stock in position. The springs exert force on the work while it is being machined. (Drawing courtesy of Sears, Roebuck & Co.)

clamp hooks to countersunk eye bolts, which are positioned in four locations on the front table. (See Illus. 1-73.) The table clamp holds small pieces securely and allows you to keep your hands well away from the blade.

The table clamp can be also used to hold

Illus. 1-71. *The Ripstrate holds stock down and against the fence during rip cuts. It can be used for both in-ripping and out-ripping. (Photo courtesy of Fisher Hill Products.)*

Illus. 1-72. *The Shophelper hold-down holds stock down on the table and in against the fence. The wheels turn only in the direction of feed. The wheels travel in a metal track and can be adjusted to the diameter of the blade or dado head. The metal track is screwed to the wooden fence.*

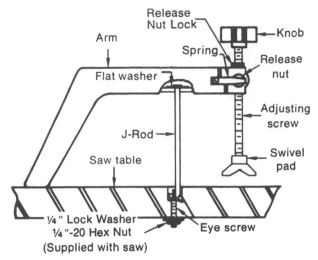

Illus. 1-73. *This table clamp locks to an eyebolt and holds stock against the fence and/or table during a crosscut. Make sure that stock is clamped securely before making a cut. (Drawing courtesy of Sears, Roebuck, & Co.)*

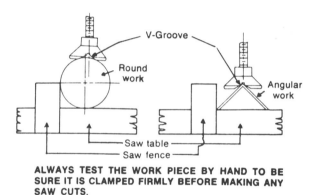

ALWAYS TEST THE WORK PIECE BY HAND TO BE SURE IT IS CLAMPED FIRMLY BEFORE MAKING ANY SAW CUTS.

Illus. 1-74. *The table clamp will also hold irregular shapes in position for crosscutting, and will allow you to keep your hands well away from the blade while the cut is being made. (Drawing courtesy of Sears, Roebuck, & Co.)*

pieces with irregular edges or shapes. Stock that cannot be clamped to the fence can be clamped to the table. The V-shaped groove helps ensure positive clamping. Note in Illus. 1-74 how the V groove is offset slightly on round stock. This forces the work against the fence. There are other devices that can be used to hold irregular pieces.

The table clamp is designed for tables at least 1 inch thick. It can be used on thinner tables if an auxiliary table is also used. Drill holes in the auxiliary table where the eyebolts are located and secure it to the front table. The auxiliary table keeps the top of the eyebolts from being higher than the top of the table.

Always check your work after clamping. The work should not move. Readjust the clamp if necessary.

Push Sticks

The push stick is a shop-made device. It is used to feed stock through the blade or cutter. It can also be used to hold stock against the fence or table. The push stick keeps your fingers clear of the blade and allows you to cut thin or narrow pieces safely.

Push sticks can be made in many different sizes and shapes. They are cut for the job at hand, usually with a sabre saw, jig saw, or band saw. This is because of their curved or irregular shapes.

Note: Before doing any sawing, cut several push sticks and keep them near the saw. Plywood scrap makes good push sticks. Many serious accidents can be avoided by using push sticks.

Chapter 7 contains patterns and instructions on how to make push sticks. Use these exact patterns or modify them to suit your needs. Be sure to round all edges and avoid sharp corners on the push sticks you make. Sharp edges and corners can easily split your skin if they are forced into your hand by a kickback.

Dead Man

The dead man or roller support is a device used to support long or wide stock being machined on the radial arm saw. There are many different types of support. Some are commercial, and others are shop-made.

Commercial supports are usually made of metal. Their height is adjustable, and they have a rolling device to support the stock. (See Illus.

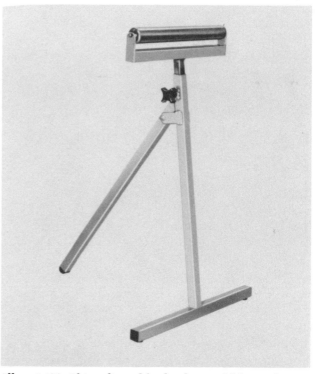

Illus. 1-75. *This adjustable dead man folds so that it can be stored away. The lock knob clamps the unit at the desired height. (Photo courtesy of HTC Products.)*

1-75 and 1-76.) Shop-made supports can also have a rolling device made of pipe, closet rod, furniture glides, or a rolling pin. The shop-made dead man may be adjustable or fixed.

Some shop-made dead-man devices are much simpler. They consist of a portable workbench sawhorse with a piece of stock or a roller. The support or dead man is adjusted at the correct height to support the stock. For occasional use, this simple dead man is enough, but, for frequent use, a better one should be made.

Built-On Tables

Built-on tables are tables added to the front or side(s) of the front table on the radial arm saw. These tables are designed to extend the working surface in one or more directions. Most often, they are adjusted so that they are in the same plane as the front table. This increases your control over long or wide pieces of stock.

Illus. 1-76. *The dead man holds the work at the desired height. The roller allows easy movement or alignment of the work.*

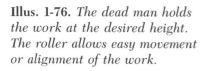

Built-on tables can be either stationary or portable. Stationary tables are permanently attached to the table. Permanent tables are usually mounted on a saw that is used chiefly for crosscutting. These tables may be smooth or they may be made up of a series of rollers.

Roller tables allow easy movement of stock for crosscutting and other operations. They also reduce friction between the stock and table. Since there is space between the rollers, sawdust does not accumulate on these tables. Sawdust accumulation between the table and the work can lift the work out of a true plane.

Smooth tables are usually made out of sheet stock. They are much less expensive than roller tables, but they have some disadvantages, such as sawdust accumulation and increased friction. They have to have adequate support or they will warp or twist out of a true plane.

Portable built-on tables can be easily removed for ripping or other setups. (See Illus. 1-77.) A portable table can be completely removable, or it can fold down next to the saw. Those which are completely removable usually have some quick-disconnect fastening such as a wing nut. Some radial-arm-saw owners have only one portable table with three quick-disconnect mounts. The mounts are located at the front and back ends of the front table. This allows the table to be quickly and easily moved to any position.

When the radial arm saw is used for ripping, usually no table is located on the feed end. This

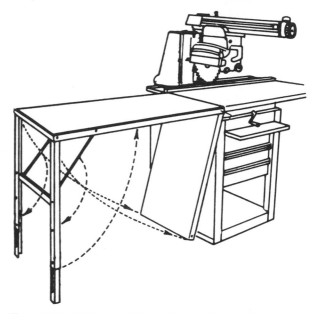

Illus. 1-77. *This portable table can be easily removed. It can be folded down and out of the way when it is not being used. (Drawing courtesy of Sears, Roebuck, & Co.)*

allows the operator to stand closer to the saw and have greater control over the operation. If the pieces are long, a table is usually mounted on the opposite end. This gives the stock additional support when the cut is completed.

If you do a great deal of ripping, use portable tables. This allows you to rip from either end and still support the stock as you finish the cut. A dead man can also be used for this purpose, but it provides much less stock control.

Mitring Jig

The mitring jig is an accessory that the operator will use to cut mitres so that he does not have to turn the arm on the saw. (See Illus. 1-78.) It even has a stop rod to control the length of the parts. (See Illus. 1-79.) The jig is attached to an auxiliary fence. The auxiliary fence is clamped in position and aligned to cut mitres.

Dust-Collection System

A portable or stationary dust-collection system should be used with all radial arm saws. Most radial-arm-saw manufacturers sell dust chutes that will collect dust behind the blade and guard. (See Illus. 1-80.) Connect the chute to a dust-collection system to gather the dust and chips at the source. (See Illus. 1-81.)

A dusty shop is a hazard. It could have a detrimental effect on your respiratory system. At the very least, use a dust mask. (See Illus. 1-82.)

Portable Bases

Portable bases are a popular radial-arm-saw accessory. Portable bases fit between the saw and the floor. They are equipped with small wheels which make the saw easy to move. The wheels can be locked to keep the saw from moving once it is in position. (See Illus. 1-83.)

The portable base raises the saw about one inch. The easy-rolling wheels make the saw easier to move and reduce the chance that movement will take the saw out of alignment.

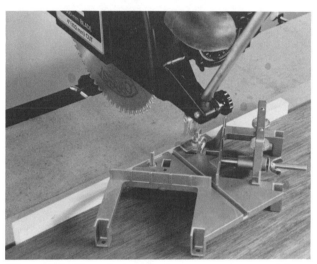

Illus. 1-78. *The mitring jig is an accessory used by the operator to cut mitres so that he does not have to turn the blade or arm of the saw. It is screwed to an auxiliary fence, which clamps between the table boards.*

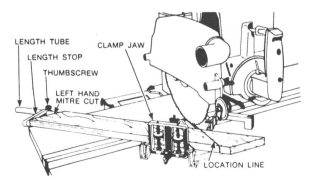

Illus. 1-79. *The mitring jig is equipped with a stop rod and clamp to increase its accuracy. (Drawing courtesy of Sears, Roebuck, & Co.)*

Illus. 1-80. *Dust chutes collect dust behind the blade. The chute can divert dust and chips towards a collection system.*

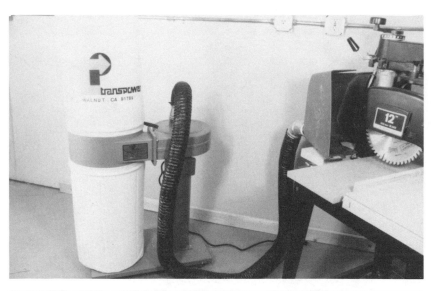

Illus. 1-81. *A dust-collection system removes dust and chips from the work environment. This makes the work area a much healthier place to work in.*

Illus. 1-82. *Protect your respiratory system with a dust mask if no dust-collection system is available.*

Illus. 1-83. *A portable base makes it easy to move the saw around the shop. This is desirable if you are working in a garage or recreation area. Once you have located the proper place for the saw, lock the wheels to keep the saw from moving.*

Chapter 2

BLADES

It is essential that you use the proper blade for the job at hand. This chapter contains the information needed to make such a selection. Two areas are explored: the factors that play a part in the selection process, and the types of blade available from which to choose.

Blade-Selection Factors

There are several factors that must be considered when you are trying to determine the proper circular-saw blade to use. These factors include tooth style and configuration, the saw's power and tolerances, the wood being cut, and the type and diameter of the saw blade. Let's explore these factors.

Friction

Consider what would happen in some cases if you were to use a fine blade. A fine blade has more teeth in the wood during the cut than a coarse blade. Since the teeth are smaller, they take a smaller bite. This decreases the rate at which the stock is fed, which means an increase in friction.

Friction is the cause of most sawing problems. It can overwork the motor and cause burning on both edges of the saw kerf (cut). Regardless of

how smooth the cut is, burning will ruin its appearance and reduce the gluing strength of the edge of the stock.

Carbide-tipped blades are the most common type of blade used on a radial arm saw. Carbide-tipped blades have teeth made from small pieces of carbide. A carbide-tipped blade will generate more friction than a tool-steel blade. (A tool-steel blade is made entirely of a very hard steel.) This is because the clearance on a tool-steel blade is obtained by bending or offsetting the teeth. (See Illus. 2-1.) This is known as **set**. The set on a tool-steel blade touches a small area in the kerf, so friction is low. In thick materials, a tool-steel blade might actually reduce friction enough to improve the cut.

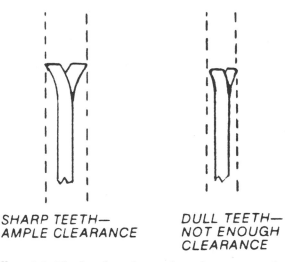

SHARP TEETH—
AMPLE CLEARANCE

DULL TEETH—
NOT ENOUGH
CLEARANCE

Illus. 2-1. *The bend in the teeth is the set. Set allows clearance for the blade as it travels through the kerf. (Drawing courtesy of Foley Belsaw.)*

Carbide-Tipped Blade A blade with teeth made from small pieces of carbide. Carbide-tipped blades are much harder and more brittle than the steel used for conventional blades. They are also more expensive, but require much less maintenance. Carbide-tipped blades come in the following classifications: rip, cross-cut, combination hollow-ground, and plywood.

Chip-Limiting Blade A type of carbide-tipped blade in which the teeth extend slightly beyond the saw rim of the plate. This is a safety feature because it limits the size of the bite the teeth take, and reduces the chance of kickback.

Coarse Blade A blade with large teeth, designed for heavy, fast, or less delicate work.

Crosscut Blade A blade that cuts across the grain. Crosscut blades have smaller teeth than rip blades. These teeth come to a point, not an edge.

Deflection (Blade) A condition in which the circular-saw blade bounces away from the workpiece.

Fine Blade A blade with small teeth, designed for more delicate work.

Footprint (Blade) Amount of blade engaged with the workpiece.

Friction The amount of resistance caused by contact between the sides of the blade and the saw kerf.

Gullet Area behind the cutting edge of the tooth. It carries away the sawdust cut by the tooth. The larger the tooth, the larger the gullet.

Heel A condition in which the front and back of the blade are not in the same plane.

Hollow-Ground Blade (also called Planer Blade) A blade with no set. The sides of the blade are recessed for clearance in the kerf. Hollow-ground blades should be used to cut mitres and compound mitres, but not used for heavy rip cuts.

Hook Angle The angle of the tooth's cutting edge as it relates to the centerline of the blade.

Kerf The cut made by a circular-saw blade. The kerf must be larger than the saw-blade thickness.

Kickback A condition in which a piece of stock is flung back at the operator at great speed. Usually, the stock becomes trapped between the rotating blade and a stationary object such as a fence or guard.

Melamine A plastic material that has been laminated to a piece of sheet stock.

Particleboard Sheet material made from wood chips or wood particles.

Pitch A wood resin that accumulates on a circular-saw blade when it becomes hot.

Resins Material within the wood which can build up on sides of the blade.

Rip Blade A blade with a straight cutting edge that is designed to cut with the grain. Rip blades have deep gullets and large hook angles.

Runout The amount that one surface is not true with another surface, or any deviation from a true orbit.

Tear-out (Grain) A condition in which the blade rips or tears out the grain of a workpiece. Tear-out can occur on the back, top, or bottom of a workpiece.

Tooth Set The bend in the blade's teeth that allows the blade to cut a kerf that is larger than the blade's thickness.

Tool-Steel Blade A circular-saw blade that is made entirely of steel.

Table 2-1. *A clarification of the terms referred to in this chapter and in the following pages.*

When cutting stock that is getting progressively thicker, you will note that more of the blade's teeth will bite into the wood. This reduces the feed rate and increases friction, which, in turn, taxes the saw motor. The solution is to replace the blade with a coarse blade, one that does not have as many teeth. As a general guideline, 3 to 5 of the blade's teeth should be in the wood during the cut.

If you tilt the blade, friction will also increase. For example, if the blade you are using has five teeth in the work and you tilt the blade so that it is at a 45-degree angle to the work, it will now have seven teeth in the wood, and the stock will be 1.4 times as thick.

Horsepower

The horsepower of a radial arm saw can affect sawing efficiency. A radial arm saw needs at least 1.5 actual horsepower to cut efficiently. If your saw has less than 1.5 horsepower, consider using a smaller-diameter blade.

If you own a 10-inch saw, consider mounting an 8-inch-diameter blade on the saw. The smaller blade requires less energy to turn, so there is more energy left to cut wood.

If you were to use an 8-inch-diameter blade on a 10-inch saw, the peripheral speed (rim speed) of the blade will decrease, so you will be feeding the stock a little slower. In such a case, select a coarser blade to compensate for the slower feed rate.

One drawback of using a smaller-diameter blade is that it will not cut as deeply as a larger blade, but most woodworkers rarely need the full depth of the blade. In those rare cases when the full depth is needed, change to a larger blade.

One additional advantage of the smaller-diameter blade is reduced blade deflection. (When a blade deflects, it bounces away from or flutters in the workpiece.) If the arbor of the saw has a .002-inch runout, deflection will be more obvious at the tip of a 10-inch blade. The further the tip of the blade is from the runout, the more

noticeable deflection becomes. Poorly toleranced saws actually work better with a smaller-diameter blade.

Guidelines for Selecting and Using Blades

Following are general guidelines concerning blades that you will find helpful when determining which blades to use. Remember, these are general guidelines. There are always exceptions.

1. Harder woods require a slower feed speed, which means that blades used in such cases will develop more heat. One way to minimize the heat buildup is to increase feed speed by using coarser blades or taking lighter cuts. A blade with 3 to 5 of its teeth in the wood is ideal.

2. Softer woods can tolerate more teeth because they have less feed resistance.

3. Smaller-diameter blades require less energy to turn, so there is more energy to cut wood. Smaller-diameter blades also run truer because arbor runout is not so pronounced.

4. Tool-steel blades generate less friction than carbide-tipped blades. This is because there is less metal contacting the sides of the saw kerf.

5. Tool-steel blades will become dull faster than carbide-tipped blades. Tool-steel blades cannot be used on materials with high-glue content such as particleboard and fibre-core plywood. The glues used on these materials are so hard that they actually take the edge off a tool-steel blade in one cut.

6. If two carbide-tipped blades with an equal number of teeth are available, remember that

BLADES

A dull blade will cause slow, inefficient cutting and an overload on the saw motor. It is a good practice to keep extra blades on hand so that sharp blades are available while the dull ones are being sharpened. (See "SAWS—SHARPENING" in Yellow Pages.) In fact, many lower-priced blades can be replaced with new ones at very little cost over the sharpening price.

Hardened gum on the blade will slow down the cutting. This gum can best be removed with trichlorethylene, kerosene or turpentine.

The following types of blade can be used with your saw:

COMBINATION BLADE—This is the latest-type fast-cutting blade for general service ripping and crosscutting. Each blade carries the correct number of teeth to cut chips rather than scrape sawdust.

CHISEL-TOOTH COMBINATION—Chisel-tooth blade edge is specially designed for general-purpose ripping and crosscutting. Fast, smooth cuts. Use of maximum speed in most cutting applications.

FRAMING/RIP COMBINATION—A 40-tooth blade for fascia, roofing, siding, sub-flooring, framing, form cutting. Rips, crosscuts, mitres, etc. Gives fast, smooth finishes when cutting with the grain of both soft and hard woods. Popular with users of worm-drive saws.

CROSSCUT BLADE—Designed specifically for fast, smooth crosscutting. Makes a smoother cut than the Combination Blade listed above.

RIP BLADE—Fast for rip cuts. Minimum binding and better chip clearance given by large teeth.

PLYWOOD BLADE—A hollow-ground, hard-chromed surface blade especially designed for exceptionally smooth cuts in plywood.

PLANER BLADE—This blade makes both rip and crosscuts. Ideal for interior woodwork. Hollow ground to produce the finest-possible saw-cut finish.

FLOORING BLADE—This is the correct blade to use on jobs when occasional nails may be encountered. Especially useful in cutting through flooring, sawing reclaimed lumber and opening boxes.

METAL-CUTTING BLADE—Has teeth shaped and set for cutting aluminum, copper, lead, and other soft metals.

FRICTION BLADE—Ideal for cutting corrugated, galvanized sheets and sheet metal up to 16 gauge. Cuts faster, with less dirt, than abrasive disc. Blade is taper-ground for clearance.

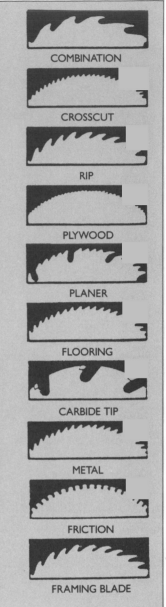

COMBINATION

CROSSCUT

RIP

PLYWOOD

PLANER

FLOORING

CARBIDE TIP

METAL

FRICTION

FRAMING BLADE

Table 2-2. *Use this chart to select the proper tool-steel blade for the job you are doing. (Drawing courtesy of Sears, Roebuck & Co.)*

the blade with the larger gullets (openings in front of the teeth) will cut the faster.

7. Friction in the saw cut is usually caused by the blade, but it may also be caused by misalignment. Make sure that the fence and blade are parallel when making a rip cut. Any misalignment can cause friction.

If both sides of the saw kerf are burned, the blade being used is probably too fine. If only the fence side is burned, the fence is probably pinching the stock against the blade. If stock tends to creep into the blade when it is being crosscut, the blade is not parallel to the path of the carriage. Check your owner's manual for alignment specifics.

8. When you tilt the blade, you increase friction because you are in effect making the cut deeper; this engages more of the blade's teeth in the wood and reduces feed speed.

9. For maximum efficiency, use the coarsest blade that produces adequate results.

Carbide-Tooth Geometry

There are two basic types of blade used for radial arm saws: tool-steel and carbide-tipped blades. Carbide-tipped blades are used more frequently. The teeth of carbide-tipped blades are designed to cut efficiently. They come in one of four configurations: alternate top bevel, alternate top bevel and raker, triple chip, or flat top. (See Illus. 2-2.) Each shape has a special cutting function.

Alternate top-bevel teeth are designed primarily for crosscutting, although they are also used for rip cuts. When they are used for rip cuts, the feed rate is less than ideal. Alternate top-bevel teeth come to a point on alternate sides of the blade. The points cut the edges of the kerf before the middle of the kerf is cut. This reduces the chance that the fibres of the stock will be torn out by the blade.

If you plan to make rip cuts and crosscuts, use a blade with alternate top-bevel and raker teeth. The alternate top-bevel teeth ensure good results when you are crosscutting, and the raker tooth (which has a flat top) cleans out the kerf during rip cuts. It actually rakes out the chips and increases feed rate. The raker tooth is slightly lower than the alternate top-bevel teeth. This prevents the raker tooth from causing tear-out during a crosscut.

A blade with triple-chip teeth is designed for cutting plywood, particleboard, melamine board, and other wood-based sheet stock. On these blades, one tooth is a flat-top tooth, and the next tooth looks like a flat-top tooth with the corners cut off. The tooth with the corners cut off separates the kerf, and the flat-top tooth planes the sides for a smooth, tear-out-free cut. These teeth resist the abrasive glues and resins in the sheet stock. This allows the blade to remain sharp after prolonged cutting of sheet stock.

Blades with triple-chip teeth can also be used for cutting solid stock, but generally they are not as efficient as blades with alternate top-bevel or alternate top-bevel and raker teeth.

Blades with flat-top teeth have only one func-

Four Popular Tooth Designs

Flat Top Grind (FT). Generally, for cutting material with grain. Larger gullets on this type blade accept greater chip loads; permit higher feed rates. Excellent for ripping on either single or multi-rip machines where speed of cut is more important than quality of cut. Teeth with square or flat top shape act as chisels, cutting material with chisel-like action. Also serve as rakers to clean out the cuttings or chips.

Triple Chip & Flat Grind (TC&F). Recommended for cutting brittle and/or hard, abrasive-type materials. Two shapes of teeth— alternate triple-edge and flat top design for dual action cutting. Triple-edge teeth chip down center of kerf; flat top raker teeth follow to clean out material from both sides. TC&F blades with negative hook angle are also recommended for cutting non-ferrous metals. Negative hook angle prevents climbing; gives you total control over the feed rate.

Alternate Top Bevel Grind (ATB). For across-the-grain cutting and/or cut-off and trimming operations on undefined grain work. Top bevel shaped teeth sever the material with shearing action alternately left and right. Given a choice, the ATB blade with the higher number of teeth will produce the higher quality of finish cut. Where finish is no concern, select the blade with fewer teeth.

Alternate Top Bevel & Raker (ATB&R). Excellent for cutting operations both with and/or across the grain. Achieves a fairly high level of quality over wide range of cuts. Two sets of shearing-action alternate left and right top bevel teeth followed by a raking action flat top tooth with large round gullet to facilitate chip removal.

Illus. 2-2. *Note the common tooth designs used on carbide-tipped blades. Each tooth design is discussed* *under the illustration. (Drawing courtesy of Delta International Machinery Corporation)*

tion: ripping. Since the wood fibres go the long way in a board, the flat-top teeth rip the wood smoothly. The quality of the cut diminishes greatly when a blade with flat-top teeth is used for crosscutting.

The first carbide-tipped blade you select for your saw should be 8 to 10 inches in diameter, with 24 to 60 teeth. For general-duty work, consider a 10-inch blade with 40 to 50 alternate top-bevel or alternate top-bevel and raker teeth, but make your final decision according to the diameter of your saw and the type of work you are doing. Buy only what you need; add blades as the job presents itself. Review the section Guidelines for Selecting and Using Blades on pages 41 and 42.

Chip-Limiting Blades

The teeth on some carbide-tipped blades extend slightly beyond the saw rim of the plate. (See Illus. 2-3.) This slows the feed rate because it limits the size of the bite the teeth can take. This also reduces the chance of kickback because each tooth has such a small grip on the work. (See Illus. 2-4.)

Illus. 2-3. *The teeth on this Credo blade extend slightly beyond the saw rim or plate. This limits the size of the bite made by the tooth and controls the cut.*

Edge of blade rises near tooth positioning the wood for a precise cut. Tips made of Tungsten Carbide, one of the hardest substances made by man.

Illus. 2-4. *The teeth are limited by the rim of the blade. This reduces the bite and the chance of kickback.*

Chapter 3

SAFETY PROCEDURES

Both the novice and experienced operator can have accidents with the radial arm saw. The novice operator's accident is usually caused by a lack of knowledge of proper safety procedures. He is not able to anticipate a potential hazard or identify an accident-producing situation. The experienced operator's accident is usually caused by either carelessness or an outright violation of the safety rules. When an experienced operator attempts and gets away with safety-rule violations, these violations soon become common practice. This is when an accident is likely to occur.

The radial arm saw has many locks, clamps, jigs, and devices that must be considered when it is set up for any job. Operators frequently forget to check *every* aspect of the setup before they begin. (See Illus. 3-1.) This can produce a hazardous condition or accident. It can also waste time and material. Rushing into the operation can cause problems.

Develop a habit of checking the setup every time you use the saw. Double-check every setting and adjustment before beginning. Check them periodically as you work.

The radial arm saw is capable of doing many jobs without a saw blade. When you are working without a saw blade, there is just as much chance of an accident occurring. These accidents could be as severe as those caused by a saw blade. Whatever attachment or jig you use, read the manufacturer's directions and safety precautions. Also consult the text in this book. Safety rules for various operations are examined when each operation is first presented.

Illus. 3-1. *Check every aspect of the radial-arm-saw setup before beginning the cut. This includes checking all locks, clamps, accessories, and jigs.*

Causes of Accidents

All accidents have contributing factors, among which are the following:

1. *Working while tired or taking medication.* Accidents are most likely to happen when you are tired. Whenever you are tired, stop or take a break. Medication and alcohol can affect your perception or reaction time.

2. *Rushing the job.* Trying to finish a job in a hurry leads to errors and accidents. The stress of

rushing the job also leads to early fatigue. If you injure yourself or make a mistake while rushing the job, the job will take far longer than it would if you worked at a normal pace.

3. *Inattention to the job.* Daydreaming or thinking about another job while working with the radial arm saw can lead to accidents. Be doubly careful when making repetitive cuts, for they can lead to daydreaming. (See Illus. 3-2.)

4. *Distractions.* Conversing with others, telephone calls, unfamiliar noises, and doors opening and closing are all distractions in the shop. Shut off the radial arm before speaking with someone, answering the phone, or investigating an unfamiliar noise.

5. *A dirty work area.* A dirty or cluttered work area provides tripping hazards and excess dust that can be a breathing hazard. Keep the shop and your radial arm saw clean. (See Illus. 3-3.) Use a dust-collection system to collect and dispose of the dust, to eliminate the problems associated with breathing dust. It is more pleasant and safer to work in a clean area.

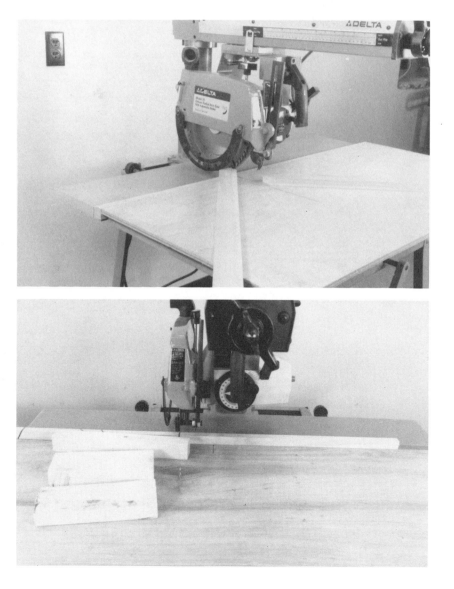

Illus. 3-2. *When making repetitive cuts with jigs such as these, it is easy to daydream. This could lead to an accident.*

Illus. 3-3. *Do not let cutoffs accumulate on the radial arm saw. They can cause accidents.*

General Working Environment

The working environment can also be a factor in the safe operation of the radial arm saw. Pay close attention to the following safety procedures, to ensure that the area you work in is a safe one:

1. Set the saw at a comfortable height. Most radial arm saws have a table height of 30 to 40 inches. Lower tables are preferred for heavy crosscuts because less lifting is required.

2. Make sure that the saw has been properly levelled and does not rock before you begin working. When possible, anchor the saw to the floor.

3. A grounded outlet of the proper voltage and correct amperage should be close by. The outlet should be below the saw so that the cord does not interfere with the stock when it is being cut or handled.

4. Make sure that the work area is well-lit. Adequate lighting makes the operation of the saw much safer. Shadows and dim lighting increase operator fatigue and measurement errors.

5. Make sure that the area surrounding the radial arm saw is large enough to accommodate large pieces of stock. If space is at a premium, use folding tables or a dead man for support.

6. Route traffic away from the saw, especially when you make a rip cut. In the event of a kickback, traffic around the radial arm saw could increase the chance of injury.

7. Keep the floor around the radial arm saw free of cutoffs and debris. Cutoffs and debris can cause tripping or slipping. Keep a box for cutoffs under the saw.

Radial-Arm-Saw Operating Rules

1. *Become familiar with how the saw works.* Complex operations require several adjustments of the radial arm saw. To work safely, you must know what the adjustments are and how to make them in the correct sequence. The owner's manual will help you understand your radial arm saw.

Many radial-arm-saw manufacturers offer general lists of safety precautions. (See Table 3-1.) Study these lists. Not all will pertain specifically to your saw, but all provide information on how to work safely with radial arm saws and other tools.

2. *Protect yourself.* Always wear protective glasses when operating the radial arm saw. If the area is noisy, wear ear plugs or muffs to preserve your hearing and minimize fatigue. (See Illus. 3-4.) Gloves are all right for handling rough lumber, but *never* wear gloves (or other loose clothing) when operating the radial arm saw. Your hands could easily be pulled into the blade if the blade caught the glove (or other loose clothing). Also, remove rings and other jewelry.

In addition, wear a dust mask or use a dust-collection system. Studies have found a high incidence of nasal cancer in woodworkers. This incidence among woodworkers is *far* higher than that of the normal population. Dust masks or collection systems are especially important when you are machining treated timbers or composition boards.

3. *Use the guards.* Use the upper guard for all operations. Never work without it. In addition, whenever possible use the lower guard in conjunction with the upper guard. The lower guard makes contact with the blade almost impossible.

Always use the splitter and anti-kickback pawls on the upper guard when making rip cuts. They will minimize the chance of kickbacks.

1. **FOR YOUR OWN SAFETY, READ INSTRUCTION MANUAL BEFORE OPERATING THE TOOL.** Learn the tool's application and limitations as well as the specific hazards peculiar to it.

2. **KEEP GUARDS IN PLACE** and in working order.

3. **GROUND ALL TOOLS.** If tool is equipped with three-prong plug, it should be plugged into a three-hole electrical receptacle. If an adapter is used to accommodate a two-prong receptacle, the adapter lug must be attached to a known ground. Never remove the third prong.

4. **REMOVE ADJUSTING KEYS AND WRENCHES.** Form habit of checking to see that keys and adjusting wrenches are removed from tool before turning it "ON."

5. **KEEP WORK AREA CLEAN.** Cluttered areas and benches invite accidents.

6. **DON'T USE IN DANGEROUS ENVIRONMENT.** Don't use power tools in damp or wet locations, or expose them to rain. Keep work area well lighted.

7. **KEEP CHILDREN AND VISITORS AWAY.** All children and visitors should be kept a safe distance from work area.

8. **MAKE WORKSHOP CHILDPROOF**—with padlocks, master switches, or by removing starter keys.

9. **DON'T FORCE TOOL.** It will do the job better and be safer at the rate for which it was designed.

10. **USE RIGHT TOOL.** Don't force tool or attachment to do a job for which it was not designed.

11. **WEAR PROPER APPAREL.** No loose clothing, gloves, neckties, rings, bracelets, or other jewelry that can get caught in moving parts. Nonslip footwear is recommended. Wear protective hair covering to contain long hair.

12. **ALWAYS USE SAFETY GLASSES.** Also use face or dust mask if cutting operations are dusty. Everyday eyeglasses only have impact-resistant lenses; they are NOT safety glasses.

13. **SECURE WORK.** Use clamps or a vise to hold work when practical. It's safer than using your hand and frees both hands to operate tool.

14. **DON'T OVERREACH.** Keep proper footing and balance at all times.

15. **MAINTAIN TOOLS IN TOP CONDITION.** Keep tools sharp and clean for best and safest performance. Follow instructions for lubricating and changing accessories.

16. **DISCONNECT TOOLS** before servicing and when changing accessories such as blades, bits, cutters, etc.

17. **USE RECOMMENDED ACCESSORIES.** Consult the owner's manual for recommended accessories. The use of improper accessories may cause hazards.

18. **AVOID ACCIDENTAL STARTING.** Make sure switch is in "OFF" position before plugging in power cord.

19. **NEVER STAND ON TOOL.** Serious injury could occur if the tool is tipped or if the cutting tool is accidentally contacted.

20. **CHECK DAMAGED PARTS.** Before further use of the tool, a guard or other part that is damaged should be carefully checked to ensure that it will operate properly and perform its intended function—check for alignment of moving parts, binding of moving parts, breakage of parts, mounting, and any other conditions that may affect its operation. A guard or other part that is damaged should be properly repaired or replaced.

21. **DIRECTION OF FEED.** Feed work into a blade or cutter against the direction of rotation of the blade or cutter only.

22. **NEVER LEAVE TOOL RUNNING UNATTENDED. TURN POWER OFF.** Don't leave tool until it comes to a complete stop.

23. **DRUGS, ALCOHOL, MEDICATION.** Do not operate tool while under the influence of drugs, alcohol or any medication.

24. **MAKE SURE TOOL IS DISCONNECTED FROM POWER SUPPLY** while motor is being mounted, connected or reconnected.

Table 3-1. *Study the safety practices listed by radial-arm-saw manufacturers, such as the ones shown here. They will help you work safely with the radial arm saw. The safety practices listed above are put out by Delta for the operation of all tools.*

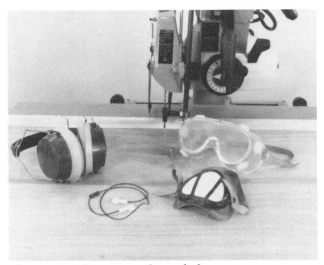

Illus. 3-4. *When using the radial arm saw, wear ear muffs or plugs, safety goggles, and a dust mask.*

4. *Keep the blade sharp.* A sharp blade makes the radial arm saw much safer to use. A dull blade increases the chance of kickback or climbing. Dull blades also require more cutting force. This excess force can throw the operator off balance and lead to an accident. It also wastes electrical energy.

To get a radial arm saw blade sharpened, consult the Yellow Pages for blade-sharpening shops.

5. *Inspect your stock.* Before sawing any stock, look it over. Loose knots, nails, twists, cupping, and rough or wet lumber can mean trouble. (See Illus. 3-5.) Loose knots can be ejec-

ted by the blade. Rough, warped, or wet lumber can cause kickbacks.

Small pieces can also prove to be dangerous. Machining them puts your hands too close to the blade. If possible, machine large pieces, and then cut them into smaller pieces.

6. *Position yourself properly.* Stand to the side of the blade to avoid kickbacks when making rip cuts. When crosscutting, make sure that the arm that pulls the carriage is slightly stiff. It will then be able to resist any climbing tendency the saw may have.

Make sure you have firm footing and balance when operating the radial arm saw. Avoid overreaching, crossing your hands, or reaching under the blade.

7. *Guard against accidental starting.* Make any adjustments to the radial arm saw with the power off. It is too easy to make an adjustment error that could cause an accident when the power is on. Make repairs, perform maintenance, make setups, and install dado heads or blades with the power disconnected. (See Illus. 3-6.) Otherwise, a serious accident could occur.

8. *Use control devices.* Devices like push sticks, hold-downs, and featherboards make handling stock safer. These devices get in close to the stock and control it. Your hands are well away from the blade, in a safe position. Keep control devices near the saw at all times.

Illus. 3-5. *Inspect stock for warp, knots, or other defects. Either avoid using stock with these defects or cut around the defects.*

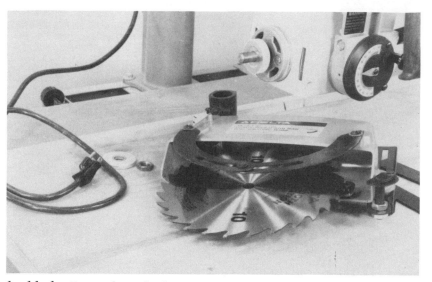

Illus. 3-6. *Make repairs, maintenance checks, setups, blade instal-
lations, and any adjustments with
the power disconnected. Accidentally starting the saw can cause
a serious injury.*

9. *Keep your hands away from the blade.* By keeping your hands a safe distance (6 to 8 inches) away from the blade, you allow a margin for error. When your hands are a safe distance from the blade, there is always time to react to a hazardous situation. Never cross your hands in front of the blade. They should be parallel to the path of the blade.

10. *Check all adjustments and devices.* Make sure all adjustments are made, all locks and clamps secured, and that the fence is clamped securely, before making any cut. Keep the carriage locked at the column when the saw is not in use.

11. *Know the path of the blade.* Make sure that you know where the blade is going when you make any cut. Keep your hands clear of the area.

12. *Think about the job beforehand.* When performing an operation, think about the job before beginning. Ask yourself, "What could happen when I . . .?" Questions of this nature help you identify and avoid an accident-producing situation. If you have a premonition of trouble, *stop.* Avoid any job that gives you a bad feeling. Try setting the job up in another way, or ask some other experienced operator for an opinion.

13. *Avoid the most common reasons for accidents.* While conversing with woodworkers who have had an accident while using the radial arm saw, I found that many were not using the lower guard, reached behind the blade during a rip cut, put their hand in the blade's path during a crosscut, or were working on a radial arm saw with a table or fence in poor repair. Most of the woodworkers involved injured their nondominant hand. This was because their dominant hand was guiding the carriage or the stock.

Crosscutting

Crosscutting, which is cutting across the grain of the wood, is the most common operation performed on radial arm saws. Although it is not hazardous, it is the most likely operation to cause an accident simply because it is so often performed. So, pay close attention to the following safety guidelines.

1. Always butt stock against the fence. (See Illus. 3-7.) When stock is not in contact with the fence, it will slam into the fence when the blade touches it. Anything between the work and the fence will be pinched (that is, jammed between the work and fence). This may also throw the radial arm saw out of adjustment.

2. Avoid stacking pieces. This can cause two or more pieces to slam together. It is safer to cut

Illus. 3-7. When crosscutting, always butt your work against the fence. Keep your hands well away from the blade when crosscutting. A lower blade guard would make the operation safer.

pieces one at a time. If the pieces *have* to be stacked, clamp them to the fence.

3. Before crosscutting round stock, be sure to clamp it to the fence or table. (See Illus. 3-8.) The stock has a tendency to turn when the blade touches it, which can cause the blade to climb the work. This can ruin the work, damage the blade, or throw the saw out of adjustment.

4. When crosscutting, use one hand to hold the work against the fence, and the other to pull the carriage. After the cut, the carriage is returned to the column and locked in position. A carriage-return spring pulls the carriage back to the column. (See Illus. 3-9.)

5. Whenever you make a crosscut, keep your arms parallel to the blade. *Never cross your arms.* This will put one arm in the blade's path. When crosscutting, keep your hands 6 to 8 inches away from the blade at all times.

6. When working with small stock, use a table clamp or other hold-down to position your work. (See Illus. 3-10.) This will keep your hands well away from the blade.

7. When working with large stock, make sure that the ends of the stock are supported. One way is to use a built-in table or a dead man. (See Illus. 3-11.) If you do not, the end of the stock could lift when you cut it. This could put your hands dangerously close to the blade.

Illus. 3-8. Before crosscutting, be sure to clamp round stock. The clamp keeps the stock from rolling into the blade.

Illus. 3-9. *The carriage-return spring pulls the carriage towards the column when the carriage is released.*

Illus. 3-10. *A table clamp makes working with small pieces much safer. Always keep your hands well away from the saw blade.*

Illus. 3-11. *Support the ends of long pieces with a built-on table or dead man when ripping or crosscutting. An unsupported piece can lift after it is cut.*

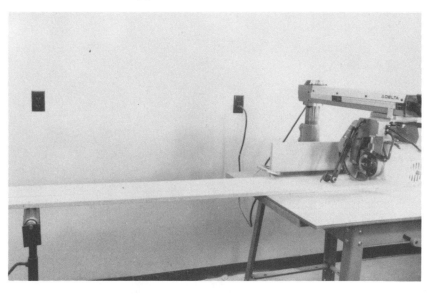

8. When doing repetitive crosscutting, keep the table free of scrap. If scrap from any operation accumulates on the saw, stop cutting, shut off the saw, and clear the table. *Clear the table only when the saw is turned off.*

Also, when doing repetitive crosscutting use a fence that is in good shape. A fence with several cuts in it can cause little scraps to pinch and be thrown away from the machine. Repetitive crosscutting is also safer when an arm clamp or stop limits carriage travel. (See Illus. 3-12.)

9. When trimming several parts, replace the fence. The new fence will keep scraps from becoming pinched between the blade and the opening in the fence. This opening should be only slightly wider than the blade. Replace the fence frequently.

10. Keep the splitter close to the surface of the stock you are crosscutting. (See Illus. 3-13.) This way, the splitter will knock your hand away from the blade should you position it incorrectly.

Crosscutting techniques are explored in Chapter 5.

Illus. 3-12. *Use an arm clamp to limit carriage travel when making repetitive cuts.*

Illus. 3-13. *Keep the splitter close to the surface of your workpiece when crosscutting. If you position your hand in the path of the blade, the splitter will knock it away.*

Ripping

Ripping, which is cutting with or along the grain of the wood, is the most dangerous of the common radial-arm-saw operations. There must be absolute control over the work during the entire ripping operation. Pay close attention to the following safety procedures:

1. Select the proper blade. This is extremely important. Blades favored for ripping on the table saw have too much hook angle for ripping on the radial arm saw. (Hook angle is explained in Chapter 2.) Table-saw rip blades have hook angles that range from 15 to 25 degrees. Radial-arm-saw blades should have less hook than this (large hook angles contribute to lifting and kickback). An angle of 0 to 15 degrees (the lower the better) is best.

It has been my experience when ripping on the radial arm saw that any of the following blades will make the job safer: Forrest Saw Woodworker 1®, DML Inc. Radi-All®, Freud LU7OM®, and the Wisconsin Knife® Nos. 08074 and 08502. Freud chip-limiting blades also reduce the chance of kickback.

All of these blades are of high quality and produce excellent results on a radial arm saw that has been set up correctly. The hook angle on these blades ranges from −6 to +15 degrees.

2. Position the nose of the guard so that it is no more than ¼ inch above the workpiece. (See Illus. 3-14.) Most guards have a warning that specifies which end of the guard *not* to rip from. Look for it on your saw.

3. Adjust the splitter so that it is properly aligned with the blade, and make sure that the anti-kickback pawls are riding on the wood. The pawls should be sharp so that they will dig into the wood in the event of a kickback. (See Illus. 3-15.) Remember that any adjustment of the guard or blade height affects the position of the pawls and splitter. If you adjust the guard, check the splitter and pawls before making a cut.

4. Because the blade orientation during ripping causes lifting of the stock and kickback problems, use hold-downs along with the guard and splitter. A commercial hold-down will help keep your hands clear of the blade. It will hold the stock down on the table and in against the fence. (See Illus. 3-16.) Also clamp a cleat to the fence to control lifting. (See Illus. 3-17.) A cleat will not hold stock in against the fence, so a featherboard should be used with it.

Illus. 3-14. *Before making rip cuts, make sure that the nose of the guard is no more than ¼ inch above the blade. This minimizes the chance of stock lifting during a rip cut.*

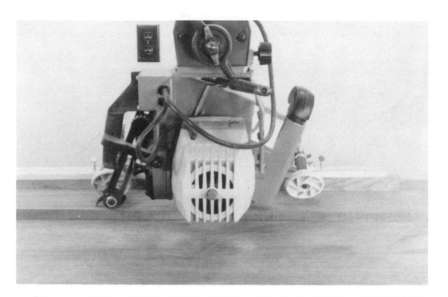

Illus. 3-15. *The pawls should ride on the work when a rip cut is being made. A sharp pawl will dig into the work and stop a kickback before any injury occurs.*

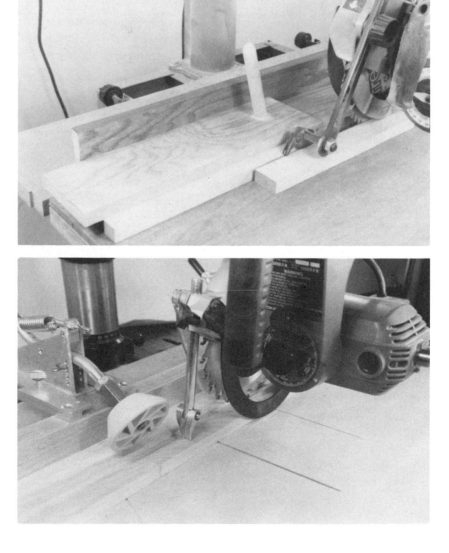

Illus. 3-16. *Commercial hold-downs can keep your hands clear of the blade. They can also guard against kickback.*

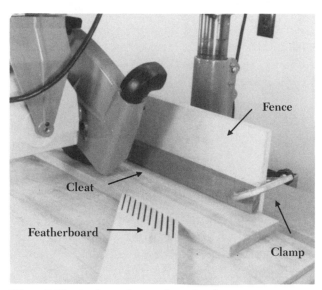

Illus. 3-17. *A cleat clamped to the fence can prevent the stock from lifting during ripping operations. A featherboard will hold stock against the fence.*

5. Pay close attention to the direction of feed. This is an important safety factor. When in-ripping, feed the stock from the right side of the saw (as you face the front of the saw). When out-ripping, feed from the left side of the saw. When in doubt, check the arrow on the guard. It will tell you which way the blade is turning. Feed the stock towards the face of the blade's teeth.

6. Keep your hands 6 to 8 inches away from the blade when making rip cuts. Use push sticks to feed stock at the end of each cut. Avoid ripping pieces shorter than 18 inches. These pieces are harder to control and bring your hands too close to the blade.

7. Also, keep your hands clear of the kickback zone in front and in back of the blade. If you are holding stock after it has been cut (behind the blade) and it kicks back, your hand could follow the wood directly into the blade. Stock over 24 inches long is the safest stock to use.

Ripping requires your full attention. Think before you cut. Efficiency is not attained by hurrying. And remember, the time put into a safe setup is time well invested.

Chapter 5 covers ripping techniques in their entirety.

Types of Accident

The two most common types of accident that oc-cur on a radial arm saw are kickbacks and broken blade teeth. Ways to eliminate or minimize these problems are explored below.

Kickbacks

A kickback occurs when a piece of stock is forced towards the operator at great speed. Usually the stock becomes trapped between a rotating blade and a stationary object such as the fence or guard. In other cases, stress in the wood causes the saw kerf to close around the blade. This traps the blade and may cause a kickback. That is why a splitter is useful. It is designed to keep the wood from closing around the blade.

Stock is kicked back at great velocity, which is very dangerous. Another danger is that the oper-ator's hand can be pulled back into the blade during a kickback if it is on the out-feed side of the blade (the side away from the operator).

You can minimize the chances that stock will kick back by observing the following precautions:

1. Cut only true, smooth stock that will not become twisted and pinched in the blade. Avoid stock with loose knots; the knots can be ejected from the wood in the same manner as a kickback. At least one edge and one face of the stock must be smooth and true. These surfaces must ride against the fence and table of the radial arm saw during the rip cut. (See Illus. 3-18.)

2. Use a guard that is equipped with a splitter and anti-kickback pawls. The splitter will keep the kerf open, and the pawls will stop the work if a kickback begins.

3. Keep the anti-kickback pawls sharp. To be effective, they must dig into the wood if a kick-back begins.

4. Use only sharp, true blades. Dull or pitch-loaded blades can cause kickbacks. (Pitch is a brown, sticky wood resin.) Warped blades also tend to pinch in the kerf and cause kickbacks. Inspect your saw blade periodically. Do this with the power disconnected.

5. When making rip cuts, select a blade with a hook angle that's under 15 degrees. Too much hook angle can cause the stock to lift or kick back.

6. Control all cuts with the fence. Never try to rip freehand or without support.

7. Avoid using the rip-cut setup for cross-cutting. Stock can get trapped between the blade and fence, and will kick back or up when the cut is completed.

8. When making rip cuts, make sure that the fence is parallel to the blade. (See Illus. 3-19.) When the fence is not parallel, stock may be pinched.

9. Always feed the piece being cut completely through and past the blade when making rip cuts. Never release the stock while it is still touching the blade and fence. A kickback may

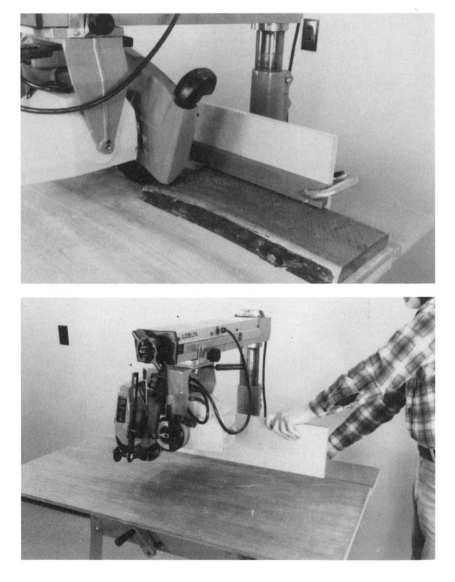

Illus. 3-18. *Stock must have at least one smooth face and one smooth edge. These surfaces must ride against the table and fence.*

Illus. 3-19. *Make sure that the fence is parallel to the blade before making a rip cut. Stock can become pinched and kick back if the fence and blade are not parallel.*

result. Use a push stick or push block for thin rip cuts. Retract the stick or block carefully after the cut has been made.

10. Stand to the side of the blade when making rip cuts. If you stand behind the piece being cut, you can become the target of a kickback. (See Illus. 3-20.)

Blade-Tip Breakage

The teeth of many radial-arm-saw blades are made of carbide. Carbide is a hard and brittle material. It is designed to resist wear caused by tough abrasive materials such as particleboard, fibre-core plywood, plastic laminates, and other sheet stock.

This hard, brittle nature also makes the carbide tips susceptible to breakage during use. Most of this breakage is the result of a sudden shock or some lateral thrust (a slap to the side of the carbide tooth). When it occurs, the carbide teeth will be propelled at great speeds.

My first experience with this problem occurred when a student cleared cutoffs from the table of a table saw with a push stick while the blade was running. When he accidentally contacted the side of the blade, a carbide tip came off. We heard a "ping" when the tip hit the fluorescent light 12 feet above.

Now, the light didn't break, and no one was injured, but I developed a new awareness of the problem. If there had been a guard on the saw and if the operator had shut off the machine before clearing the scraps, then this accident would not have happened!

Some other causes of tip breakage are foreign objects or loose knots in the wood. A panelling nail or drywall screw will usually break a few tips on the saw blade. This is because of the hardness of these objects.

A loose nail or knot will turn during the sawing operation. As it turns, it causes enough stress on the brittle carbide tip to cause it to fracture. Although a common nail usually does not move during the sawing process and can be machined, any other foreign material should be removed from the wood before it is cut.

Twisted stock can also cause problems during a rip cut. As the part twists through the blade, it may generate enough side stress to fracture a carbide tip. It is best to cut twisted stock into shorter parts where the twist is less pronounced.

Some other common causes of tip breakage are listed below:

1. Any play in the arbor or the arbor bearings that could cause lateral stress.

2. A fence or splitter that pinches on the back

Illus. 3-20. *Stand to the side of the blade when making a rip cut. Stay out of the kickback zone. Do not become a target of a kickback.*

side of the blade. This causes side stress and heat build-up at the carbide tips. Sufficient heat can soften a braze joint; that is why carbide-tipped blades should be sharpened under a coolant.

3. Operating the saw blade at a speed higher than specified on the blade. If the blade is not designed for the saw speed, centrifugal force can actually break the braze joint holding the carbide tip to the plate.

4. Operating the radial arm saw freehand. Any freehand operation on the radial arm saw can also cause tip breakage. Always control the work with the fence and table during the cut.

5. Vibration. Use a dampener or saw collars to reduce blade vibration. Make sure that the saw is firmly on the floor so that it does not rock and cause vibration. When sawing thin stock, use a featherboard or other device to ensure that it does not cause vibration while it is being cut. Ripping thin strips without the use of a splitter can also encourage tip failure. The fluttering of the thin strip can generate vibrations and side stress.

6. General care of the blades. This can also be a factor in tip damage. I have seen people pry a new blade out of its protective case with a screwdriver, only to break a tip or two.

Keeping the saw blades clean can also reduce the chance of tip damage. Pitch build-up can cause heat to build up at the tips, and it can also generate extra stress during the cut. Some forms of pitch are highly acidic and can actually break down the carbide at the cutting edge. This means that the tips are getting dull even though they are not being used.

Before mounting any carbide-tipped (or any other type) blade on the saw, look it over to be sure that it is in good condition. The braze joints should look strong, and there should be no cracks on the carbide. Clean the tips if pitch build-up makes it impossible to inspect them. Be sure that the blade can handle the arbor speed; if not, do not use that blade; find one that can.

Broken carbide tips can be replaced by a competent sharpening service, which can be found in the Yellow Pages, but the best practice is do everything possible to eliminate the chance of tip breakage. If the sharpening service has to replace and grind more than three tips, the cost can approach 30 percent or more of the cost of the blade.

Chapter 4

PRE-USE PROCEDURES

Before you can use the radial arm saw, you have to first set it up properly and then change the blade currently on the saw for the one you have selected. These procedures are described below.

Setting Up the Saw

Set up the saw *with the power disconnected.* Do the following:

1. If you are working with a bench or tabletop saw, make sure that it is clamped securely to a sawhorse or other stable object. (See Illus. 4-1.) If your saw has a commercial base, adjust the leg levellers to the floor where it will be positioned.

If the base does not have adjustable levellers, make sure that it does not rock. If it does, place a shim under the low leg. This will make sawing safer and more accurate.

2. Check that the table is square to the blade's path. (See Illus. 4-2.) (When the table is "square" to the blade, it is at right angles to it.) To do this, position a framing square over the table edge and pull the blade towards you. The blade should follow the square. Adjust the table if it is not square to the blade.

3. Check that the blade is square to the table. (See Illus. 4-3.) When doing this, make sure that the square is not on the teeth of the blade, but on the plate. This provides the most accurate read-

Illus. 4-1. *Make sure that your saw is securely clamped to a work surface before doing any sawing.*

Illus. 4-2. *Use a framing square to check that the table is square to the blade's path. Adjust the table (not the column) if the table is not square to the blade.*

Illus. 4-3. *Make sure that the blade is square to the table. Make any adjustments according to the owner's manual or by following the instructions on pages 59 and 60.*

Illus. 4-4. *An auxiliary table will protect the original table from damage. Replace the auxiliary table when it becomes damaged.*

ing. If the blade must be adjusted, release any locking part and make the adjustment. Make sure that you secure any locks after making the setting.

4. Install an auxiliary table. (See Illus. 4-4.) This will protect the original table. The auxiliary table can be replaced when it becomes cut up.

5. Install a new fence. (See Illus. 4-5.) This fence should be straight and true. Replace it when it becomes cut up.

Changing the Blade

Before changing the blade, disconnect the power. Unplug the saw or shut off the power at the main junction box. Then do the following:

1. Raise the blade so that it clears the table, and then pull the carriage towards you. Lock the carriage near the end of the stroke. (See Illus. 4-6.) This brings the blade closer to you and makes blade removal less cumbersome.

2. Release the guard's (or guards') clamping mechanism(s) and remove the guard(s). (See Illus. 4-7.) There will be one or two guards (an upper or lower).

3. Remove the arbor nut. To do this, look at the threads on the arbor. If they are right-hand

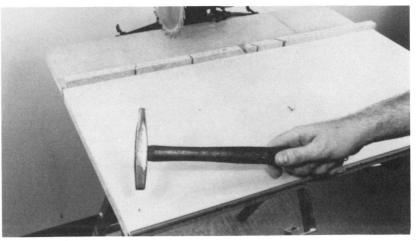

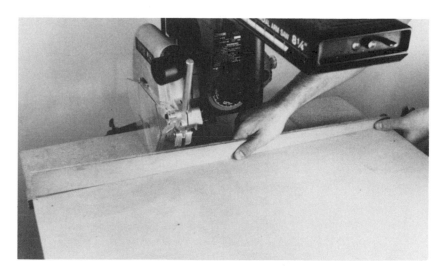

Illus. 4-5. *Make sure that the fence you install is straight and true. Replace it when it has been cut several times.*

Illus. 4-6. *To change the blade, first disconnect the power. Then raise the blade so that it clears the table, as shown here, pull the carriage towards you, and lock the carriage near the end of the stroke.*

threads, remove the arbor nut by turning it clockwise. Radial arm saws with a brass arbor nut have left-hand threads. The nut was machined out of brass so that it would be the weakest part of the arbor. It is cheaper to replace an arbor nut than to replace the arbor. However, if it is turned the wrong way (overtightened), the threads will strip.

To remove the arbor nut on most radial arm saws, you will need two wrenches. One wrench holds the arbor stationary, while the other turns the arbor nut. (See Illus. 4-8.) For some radial arm saws, you will need only one wrench to turn the arbor nut. The arbor is held stationary with a lock pin that is mounted on the motor. This spring-loaded pin is pushed down against the arbor to hold it in place. Your owner's manual can provide more specific information.

4. Pull the arbor washers (and blade stabilizers, if used) off the arbor. Inspect the arbor washers and blade stabilizers for pitch, wood chips, nicks, or dents. (See Illus. 4-9 and 4-10.) Remove any irregularity from the washers and stabilizers. The washers should bear against the saw blade uniformly at their outer edges.

5. Replace the inner blade washer (and blade stabilizers).

Illus. 4-7. *Remove the upper guard for access to the arbor nut. Note that the saw has been disconnected from its power source.*

Illus. 4-8. *You will need two wrenches to remove the arbor nut on most radial arm saws. Use one wrench to hold the arbor stationary, and the other to turn the arbor nut.*

Illus. 4-9. *After removing the blade, inspect the arbor washers and stabilizers (or dampeners) for nicks, dents, or defects.*

Illus. 4-10. *This arbor washer is ready to replace the washer that was previously on the arbor. It is clean and free of defects.*

6. Install the desired blade over the arbor. (See Illus. 4-11.) The blade's teeth should point towards the table at the front (operator's side) of the table. *Note:* If the replacement blade is larger than the one removed, it may be necessary to raise the motor using the blade-elevating crank.

7. Place the outer arbor washer (and blade stabilizer or dampener) on the arbor. (See Illus. 4-12.)

8. Replace the arbor nut. Tighten it snugly against the blade, but do not overtighten it. That can make removal very difficult. Machines that have an electronic brake put more strain on the arbor nut, so these arbor nuts should be tight-

Illus. 4-11. The desired blade (a chip-limiting, 50-tooth combination blade with alternate top bevel and raker teeth) has been positioned on the arbor. The teeth point towards the table on the operator's side of the saw. Note: On some saws, the guard must be installed with the blade.

Illus. 4-12. Put a clean outer arbor washer on the arbor against the blade, as shown here. Then install the arbor nut and tighten it securely.

ened with increased force. Otherwise, the nut could loosen when braking occurs.

9. Replace the guard(s). (See Illus. 4-13 and 4-14.) Make sure that the guard is clamped securely and adjusted correctly.

Illus. 4-13. Replace the guard. Turn the blade over by hand to be sure that it clears the guard. Do this with the power disconnected.

Illus. 4-14. The guards, blade, and arbor nut are all replaced as a unit on this saw. Tighten the arbor nut using two wrenches, as shown here.

10. Release the carriage and move it to the column.

11. Lower the blade so that it is just above the table.

12. Plug in the saw and turn it on.

13. Lock the carriage to the arm, and lower the blade slowly into the table.

14. Release the clamp and pull the carriage through its complete stroke. There should be a cut in the fence and table ⅟₁₆ to ⅛ inch deep. (See Illus. 4-15.)

Illus. 4-15. *Make a kerf or cut in the fence and table with the new blade. If either the fence or table is damaged, it should be replaced.*

It may not be necessary to kerf or make a cut on the table. If the new blade fits in the kerf cut by the previous blade, then crosscutting can begin right away. To determine if the new blade fits in the kerf cut by the previous blade, pull the carriage through its stroke before sawing. *Do this with the power off.* Make sure that everything is aligned before you begin sawing.

Using Smaller-Diameter Blades

If you use a blade that has a smaller diameter than can be used on the radial arm saw, there are certain advantages and disadvantages you should be aware of. One advantage is that this type of blade can make a more powerful cut. This is because less energy is needed to turn it, so increased power is available at the cut. Another advantage is that there will be less blade deflection. Since the blade is smaller in diameter, maximum runout (blade deviation at its periphery) is decreased. This increases blade life and improves the cut.

There are two disadvantages to using a smaller-diameter blade. First, this blade cannot cut as deeply as the larger-diameter blade. It cannot be used to make rip cuts on, or crosscut, thick stock. Instead, a larger-diameter blade should be used. Secondly, when this type of blade is used, sawdust will not be ejected and collected as efficiently. This is because the upper guard, which is designed to eject sawdust away from the cutting area, works better when used with a blade of maximum diameter. When smaller blades are used, the chips tend to fall on the work. This can sometimes damage stock that has been finish-sanded.

If you use a smaller-diameter blade, be careful. Make sure that the rpm rating for the blade is correct for your saw. Also, be aware that when a smaller blade is tilted, it will not follow the same path as a larger blade. Make sure that it does not go through a table clamp or table fastener. This could damage the blade or table.

Keep in mind that a smaller-diameter blade has a different relationship to the guard than a larger-diameter one. This can alter your perception of the blade's position and cause an error or mishap. Also, when a smaller blade is used for some cuts, the carriage does not return completely to the column. This can cause the blade to engage with the work before it should. When this happens, the blade tends to climb the work, and can throw the saw out of alignment.

Chapter 5

BASIC CUTS

Before engaging in any of the basic cutting techniques described in this chapter, pay heed to the following words of advice: Always carefully plan before any operation. Think about the job before beginning. Try to anticipate any problems before turning on the saw. And, of course, carefully re-read all the safety information presented in Chapter 3. All these procedures will make the job a safer one, and yield better results.

Ripping

Ripping is one of the most common radial-arm-saw operations. In ripping, the cut is made *with*, *or along*, the grain. The yoke is turned 90 degrees in either direction so that the blade will be parallel with the fence. The wood is then fed against the cutting rotation.

When the blade is closer than the motor to the fence, it is known as "in-ripping." When the motor is closer to the fence, it is known as "out-ripping." In-ripping is usually used for cutting narrow strips. Out-ripping is the favored setup for cutting wide parts. It allows you to make the widest possible cut on your radial arm saw.

Review the safety procedures for ripping in Chapter 3 before beginning. Begin the ripping operation by checking the blade for a condition called "heel" while it is in the crosscut position. (See Illus. 5-1). Heel occurs when the front and back of the blade are not in the same plane. Correct this before proceeding.

Illus. 5-1. *Before making any rip cuts, use a square to check the blade for heeling. Place the square against the blade. The part of the square against the blade should contact the entire plate of the blade. If it doesn't, the blade has a heeling condition. Correct this. If the blade has a heeling condition, the work can bind or will be difficult to keep against the fence. Note the chip-limiting blade being used on this saw.*

Next, turn the yoke 90 degrees and cut your rip trough. Place an auxiliary table on your saw to protect the saw table. If, however, you have set up the saw for precise rip cuts, use an auxiliary table without a rip trough. In this case, adjust the blade for rip width while it is above the table; then turn the saw on and lower the blade into the table about ⅛ inch. This helps minimize blade deflection as the cut is made.

For best results, also install a new fence. (See Illus. 5-2.) A fence with many cuts in it can catch on the work as it moves past it. This can damage your work, and may cause a kickback.

Illus. 5-2. *For best results when making rip cuts, install a new, uncut fence. The fence shown here is taller than the crosscut fence. It allows holding devices to be clamped to it.*

Turn the yoke to the rip position. (See Illus. 5-3.) Lock it in position. (See Illus. 5-4.) Move the carriage and set the distance between the blade and fence to the desired width. Measure this distance from a tooth that points towards the

Illus. 5-3. *Turn the yoke to the rip position. This setup is for in-ripping.*

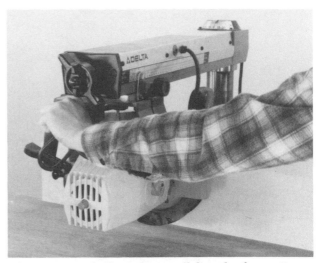

Illus. 5-4. *Lock the yoke parallel to the fence. Drop the stop pin in position before clamping the yoke.*

Illus. 5-5. *Use a ruler to set the distance between the blade and fence. This is the size of the rip cut you plan to make. Be sure to use a tooth that points towards the fence. Lock the carriage once the setting is made.*

fence. (See Illus. 5-5.) This gives the most accurate setting.

Move the upper blade guard down so that it just clears the stock. (See Illus. 5-6.) Clamp a cleat on the fence and/or use a commercial hold-down or featherboard to keep the stock from lifting during the cut. (See Illus. 5-7 and 5-8.)

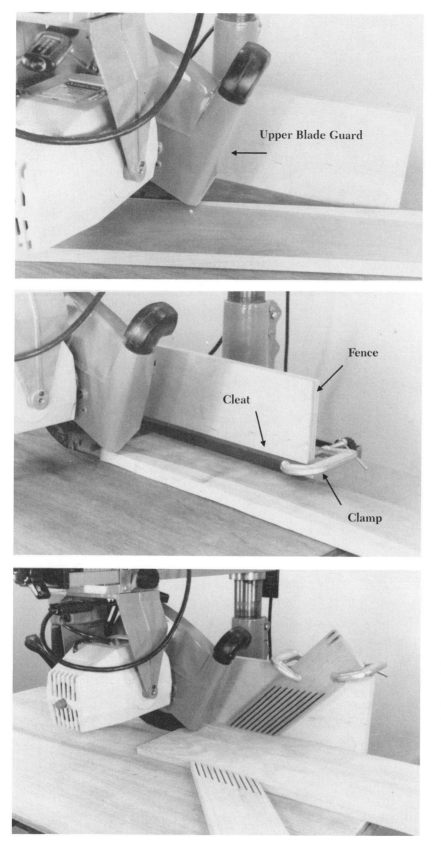

Illus. 5-6. *Tip the upper blade guard towards the in-feed end of the saw. This is the end nearer to the operator. The guard should just clear the workpiece. Clamp the guard securely.*

Illus. 5-7. *Clamp a cleat to the fence. It should just clear the stock thickness. The cleat will prevent the stock from lifting.*

Illus. 5-8. *You can clamp featherboards to the fence or table to control stock when making rip cuts.*

Drop the splitter and anti-kickback pawls into position. (See Illus. 5-9.) Use a piece of stock to position them. Clamp the splitter and pawls securely in position. The splitter and pawls help control the stock and guard against a kickback.

Illus. 5-9. *Position the splitter and anti-kickback pawls at the correct height for stock thickness. The anti-kickback pawls must dig into the wood in the event of a kickback.*

Turn on the saw, and feed the stock against the blade rotation. (See Illus. 5-10.) When in-ripping, feed the stock from the right side of the saw (as you face the front of the saw). When out-ripping, feed the stock from the left side.

Guide the stock into the blade at a uniform speed. Stand to the side of the stock so that you are clear of the kickback zone. Keep your feet about shoulder width apart. Balance your weight evenly on both feet.

If the blade slows down, either you are feeding the stock too quickly or the blade has teeth that are too fine for the stock thickness. If the edges of the saw kerf appear burned, you may be feeding the stock too slowly. This may also indicate that the blade is dull or that it is binding in the stock. If the work tends to pull away from the fence, there may be heel in the blade. Check the blade to be sure that it is parallel to the fence.

Guide the entire length of the work through the blade. (See Illus. 5-11.) Use a push stick to keep your hands clear of the blade. (See Illus. 5-12.) Do not stop feeding the stock into the blade until the entire piece is past the blade. (See Illus. 5-13.) If the piece stops while in contact with the blade and fence, a kickback could occur.

When making rip cuts on long pieces, use a dead man or other device to support the wood. (See Illus. 5-14.) Large, heavy pieces may require an extra person to handle and guide them safely. Never try to rip stock that is too heavy or large for you to handle.

When ripping strips off a piece of sheet stock, make the widest rip cut first. This puts most of the panel's weight on the radial arm saw. It also minimizes flexing in thin, lighter sheets, and gives truer cuts. It may also be beneficial to cut the length of the panel in half before making a rip cut on it.

A stock-cutting sheet allows you to plan your

Illus. 5-10. *Turn on the saw and feed the stock into the blade. Stand clear of the kickback zone. Make sure that the stock is against the fence and under the cleat.*

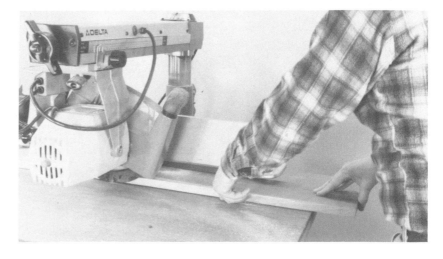

Illus. 5-11. *Guide the entire piece through the blade. The splitter and anti-kickback pawls help control the work.*

Illus. 5-12. *Use a push stick to complete the cut. The push stick helps keep your hands clear of the blade. The guards also help make the rip cuts safer.*

Illus. 5-13. *Do not stop feeding the work until it is completely clear of the blade and lower blade guard.*

Illus. 5-14. *When making rip cuts on long pieces, use a dead man to support the work. Make sure that the dead man is positioned to balance the wood.*

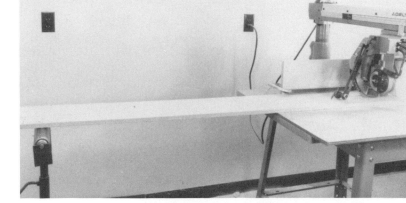

cuts before doing any cutting. Graph paper makes the layout simple. Mark off an area on the graph paper that is 4 squares by 8 squares. Sketch in the grain direction if your stock has a grain direction. Draw all the needed parts onto the graph paper, so that all cuts are organized. Number the cuts for more efficient cutting.

Remember, the outer edges of the sheet stock are true and square. These edges can always be used as control surfaces for accurate cutting.

Making Rip Cuts on Narrow Pieces

Making rip cuts on narrow pieces can be dangerous if not performed correctly. Narrow pieces tend to vibrate and flutter as they are cut. These pieces can snap in half, shatter, or kick back. It is important that appropriate hold-downs be used to prevent vibration and fluttering. A push stick should also be used. (See Illus. 5-15–5-19.)

A blade with finer teeth should be used for ripping thin, narrow strips. The finer teeth cause less vibration and fluttering. They also reduce the chance that stock will lift off the table during the cut.

Avoid ripping thin strips off pieces that are less than 18 inches long. Select an alternative method of cutting the strips. If the pieces are quite long, make sure you have a helper to pull the thin strips through. Use a push block to feed the strip beyond the saw blade unless you are using a holding device such as a Shophelper hold-down. (See Illus. 5-20.)

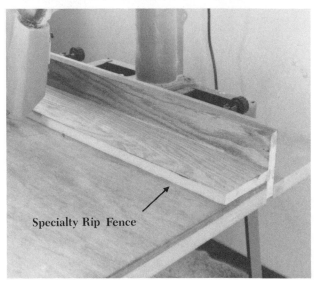

Specialty Rip Fence

Illus. 5-15. *This special fence is used to make rip cuts on narrow pieces.*

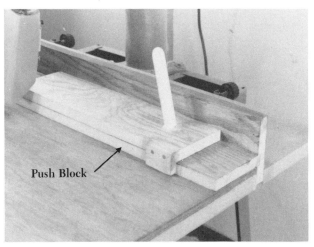

Push Block

Illus. 5-16. *A shop-made push block rides on the special fence. It controls the cut.*

Illus. 5-17. *Position the work against the push block. The face of the work should be on the table.*

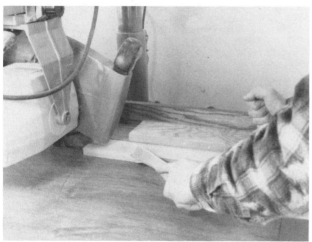

Illus. 5-18. *Use a push stick to hold the work against the push block and fence.*

Illus. 5-19. *The push block safely guides the narrow piece past the blade and lower guard.*

Illus. 5-20. *The wheels on the Shophelper hold-down hold the narrow piece against the fence while the cut is being made. This keeps the work from fluttering or vibrating.*

When retracting the push block, pull it back carefully. If you twist it, the end may be torn up by the blade, and the thin strip that does the pushing will be removed. Replace the push block if this occurs.

Crosscutting

Crosscutting is the most common cut made with the radial arm saw. In fact, some people use their radial arm saws exclusively for crosscutting. This is using the saw at about 10 percent of its potential. Before making a crosscut, carefully review the safety procedures for crosscutting in Chapter 3.

A crosscut is a cut made against the grain of the stock. Crosscutting is done by putting the edge of the work against the fence and pulling the carriage (and blade) across it. To ensure a square cut, make sure that the arm and blade are perpendicular to the fence, and that the blade is perpendicular to the table. To prevent tear-out, make sure that the blade does not heel. Make these checks before crosscutting. First, check the blade. It should be square with the fence and the table. (See Illus. 5-21.) Keep the square off the blade's teeth. Then check for heeling. (See Illus. 5-22.) Make any necessary adjustments.

Illus. 5-21. *Make sure that the blade is square with the table and fence. This will ensure that the end of the stock is perpendicular to the faces.*

Illus. 5-22. *Use a square to check the blade for heel. Heel is the chief cause of grain tear-out during crosscuts. If the square touches the entire surface of the blade while in contact with the fence, the blade does not have heel.*

Check arm tracking by placing a framing square against the fence. Line the other leg of the square up with the blade. Select a tooth and position it so that it's touching the square. Slowly pull the carriage towards you. (See Illus. 5-23.) Observe the tooth and square; if the blade begins to move, *stop* the blade. If you don't, the tooth could climb the square and break. This movement is an indication of arm misalignment. Another indication is space between the tooth and square at the end of the stroke.

Begin the crosscut by placing the work against the fence. The work should also rest firmly on the table. Support long pieces with a dead man. Line up the cut with the blade. (See Illus. 5-24.) Your layout line should line up with a tooth that points towards the layout line. The saw blade should be on the waste or scrap side of the line. The waste side is the part of the work that is being cut off.

Turn on the saw and pull the carriage (and blade) into the work. Hold the work securely with your other hand. (See Illus. 5-25). Make sure that your hand is not in the blade's path. Your hands should be parallel to the blade. Never cross your arms.

The arm pulling the carriage should be kept slightly stiff. This will keep the blade from climbing the work and jamming or throwing the saw out of alignment. This climbing is sometimes caused by a blade with too much hook.

Pull the carriage at uniform speed. If the mo-

Illus. 5-23. *Pull the carriage through its path to see if the arm is tracking properly. Make any needed adjustments before you begin crosscutting.*

Illus. 5-24. *Line up your layout line with the kerf in the fence. Make sure that the kerf is on the waste side.*

Layout Line

Fence Kerf

Illus. 5-25. *Hold the work with your other hand. Your hands should never cross. They should remain parallel to the blade's path.*

tor slows down, you are moving the carriage too fast. After the crosscut is completed, return the carriage to the column and shut off the motor. Lock the carriage in position. (See Illus. 5-26.)

Illus. 5-26. *When the cut has been completed, shut the power off and return the carriage to the column and clamp it to the arm.*

When crosscutting, keep scrap off the table. Be sure to shut the saw off before clearing the table. When the cutoff scraps are small, they sometimes become trapped between the blade and the kerf in the fence. To prevent this, install the desired blade and a new fence with one kerf cut in it. One cut in the fence will keep scrap from getting caught and will minimize tear-out. It will also make it easier to align the layout line with the blade's path. (See Illus. 5-27.)

Work wider than the stroke of the radial arm saw can be cut in two operations. First, position the stock and saw it to the end of the arm's stroke. (See Illus. 5-28.) Then flip the piece over and align it with the blade's path. (See Illus. 5-29.) Do this *with the power off.* Then complete the cut with the second stroke of the blade. (See Illus. 5-30.)

If the arm is not aligned correctly, the two cuts will not meet. Try a cut on scrap stock before attempting a cut on expensive stock or an important piece for a project you are building.

Illus. 5-27. *A clean fence with one saw kerf in it will make it easier to get accurate cuts and control tear-out. Replace the fence if it becomes damaged.*

Illus. 5-28. *Crosscut the wide piece to the end of the arm's stroke. Blade diameter and fence position will affect the length of the cut somewhat.*

Illus. 5-29. *Turn the piece over and align the cut with the blade.*

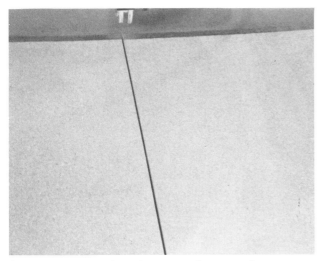

Illus. 5-30. *Complete the cut and return the carriage to the column.*

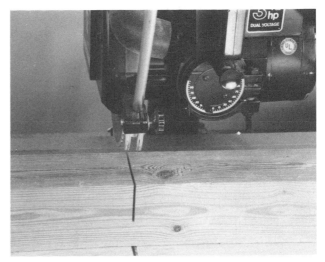

Illus. 5-32. *When stock is too thick to be cut in one stroke, cut as deep as possible on the first stroke. Make sure that the motor clears the top of the workpiece.*

Sometimes a stop is clamped to the fence or table to help align the two cuts. (See Illus. 5-31.) This will work only when the end of the piece is square. Most factory edges on plywood are square. Check solid stock with a framing square before using this method.

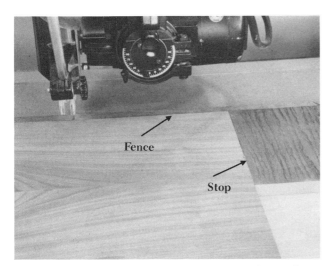

Illus. 5-31. *A plywood stop is sometimes clamped to the table to position a wide piece. The stop and the work must both be square.*

Pieces that are too thick for the blade should also be handled in two cuts. Make the first cut as deep as possible. (See Illus. 5-32.) Then turn the

piece over and complete the cut. (See Illus. 5-33.) The blade has to be square with the fence and table or the two cuts will be uneven.

Small or short pieces can also be a problem when you are crosscutting. These pieces bring your hands too close to the blade. Special clamping mechanisms can be used to hold the stock in place while the cut is being made. (See Illus. 5-34.) A holding device that engages with the

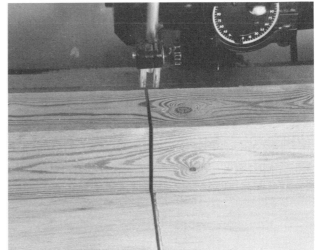

Illus. 5-33. *Turn the piece over and complete the cut with a second stroke. Line this cut up carefully.*

Illus. 5-34. *Special clamping devices can be used to keep your hands clear of the blade. This stock can be cut safely and accurately.*

fence can also be made. It will do the same job as the clamping mechanisms.

Sometimes a special fence has to be made for this operation. A fence that has a series of dadoes cut into it will do the job in most cases. (See Illus. 5-35.) (Dadoes are examined on pages 88–93 and 97–99.) You will also have to make a stick to use with the fence. The stick has an offset tongue

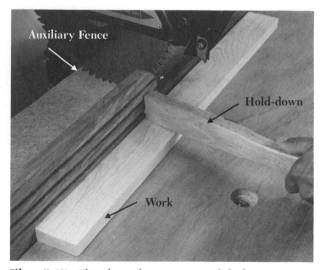

Illus. 5-35. *This fence has a series of dadoes cut into it. The holding device engages with the dadoes in the fence. It holds stock safely and keeps your hand clear of the blade's path.*

that makes it possible to hold stock of varying thicknesses. (See Illus. 5-36.)

Illus. 5-36. *The tongue on the holding device is offset. You can flip it over for stock of different thicknesses.*

The commercial hold-down shown in Illus. 5-37 hooks into eye bolts (bolts with looped ends). The knob on top produces the needed clamping pressure to hold stock in place. (See Illus. 5-38.) The V in the clamp pad will hold round and irregular pieces in place. The hold-down stays clear of the work during the cut.

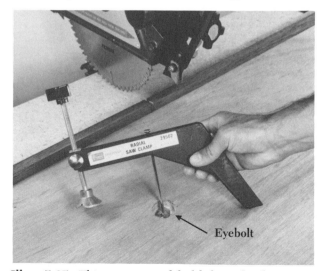

Illus. 5-37. *This commercial hold-down hooks into an eyebolt. The eyebolt replaces the standard table bolt.*

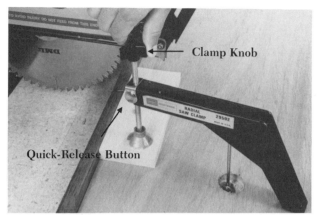

Illus. 5-38. *Turning the knob on this hold-down produces the clamping pressure. The hold-down has a quick release, for faster adjustment.*

Illus. 5-39. *Clamp round stock to the table or fence before crosscutting it. Round stock has a tendency to roll into and jam the blade. The clamp keeps it from moving.*

Round stock must be held securely when it is being crosscut. (See Illus. 5-39.) This is because it has a tendency to roll towards the blade and jam it. In addition to being dangerous, this can throw the radial arm saw out of adjustment or damage the blade. A clamp should be used to hold the round stock to the fence while you are crosscutting.

It is frequently necessary to crosscut several pieces to the same length. To eliminate layout of individual pieces, clamp a stop block to the fence or table. (See Illus. 5-40.) Set the stop block by measuring the distance from the blade. Make the measurement from a tooth that points towards the stop block. Then secure the stop block to the fence or table.

Make a test cut on scrap. The scrap does not have to be cut in half. Measure the scrap to make sure that its length is correct. Make any needed adjustments and proceed with the operation.

There are some commercial stop devices that can be secured to the fence. (See Illus. 5-41.) Minor adjustments can be made to these devices without having to remove them from the fence. Devices can be made in the workshop with less expense. (See Illus. 5-42 and 5-43.)

Whenever you use a stop block, make sure that sawdust does not accumulate between it and the work. You can prevent this problem in most cases by cutting a rabbet on the end of the stop block. (See Illus. 5-44.)

When using a stop that is clamped to the fence

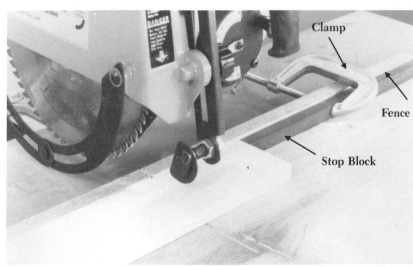

Illus. 5-40. *A stop block is frequently used to control the length of the part. Clamp the block to the table or fence.*

Illus. 5-41. *This commercial stop attaches to the fence. Minor adjustments can be made to the stop without it having to be removed from the fence.*

Illus. 5-42. *This shop-made stop has a flathead machine screw that can be used to make minor adjustments in the length of the part.*

Illus. 5-43. *Loosen the nut with a wrench and adjust the machine screw.*

Illus. 5-44. *The rabbet cut on the underside of the stop prevents sawdust from accumulating and interfering with accurate cross-cutting. Set up the cut carefully using a ruler.*

or table, handle your stock carefully. Banging the work against the stop can cause it to move slightly, which can cause the pieces to be cut at different lengths. This can spoil the work or waste time or stock. Push the work against the stop carefully and check the length of the parts periodically.

When making repetitive crosscuts, place a stop on the arm of the saw. (See Illus. 5-45.) This keeps you from pulling the carriage (and blade) further than necessary. It also makes the operation safer. The Occupational Safety and Health Administration (OSHA) requires this in industrial operations. One of the requirements is that "an adjustable stop shall be provided to prevent the forward travel of the blade beyond the position necessary to complete the cut in repetitive operations."

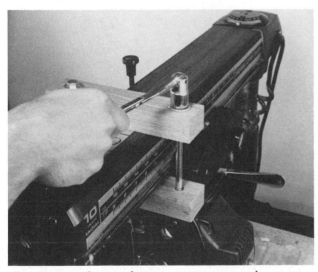

Illus. 5-45. *When making repetitive cuts, clamp a stop to the arm or track of the saw to control stroke length.*

When some materials are crosscut, grain tear-out is a problem. Tear-out usually occurs on the bottom of the piece. This is sometimes caused when the blade is pulled through the work too quickly. A slower feed may reduce or eliminate tear-out. A table with many kerf cuts will encourage tear-out. This is because the wood fibres are not supported when the blade cuts through the work. An auxiliary table should improve the cut.

Cutting Mitres

Mitres are crosscuts made at an angle. Mitres across the face of a piece (from edge to edge) are usually made by turning the arm to the left or right. Mitres across the end (from face to face) are usually made by tilting the motor in its yoke. Mitres along the edge of a piece require that the motor be tilted in the yoke, and the yoke turned 90 degrees into the rip position.

Most mitre cuts are made at a 45-degree angle, but mitres can be cut at any angle. Determine the correct or desired angle before beginning to make any adjustments.

Face Mitres

Mitres across the face of the work are commonly cut on picture-frame stock and door or window trim. To make a face mitre, the saw's arm must be turned to the right or left. Begin by checking the scale on the column. Make sure that the indicator is aligned with zero. Then release the arm clamp and pull the locking pin clear of its detent. (A detent is a device that positions and holds one mechanical part in relation to another.) Now, raise the blade out of the table kerf.

To make a right-hand mitre, turn the arm to the right. (See Illus. 5-46.) Keep your eyes on the blade to make sure that it does not touch the fence or table boards. If the desired angle is 45 degrees, the arm will lock in position. The pin will drop into a detent. Tap the pin lever with the palm of your hand to make sure it is engaged properly. Then, clamp the arm clamp securely.

The locking pin will not engage at any angle other than 45 degrees. The arm clamp is the only thing holding the setting, so make sure it is clamped securely.

The scale on the column can be used to set the mitre angle. For exact angular settings, use a sliding T-bevel. (See Illus. 5-47.) Place the head of the sliding T-bevel against the fence; this will bring the blade of the sliding T-bevel into contact with the saw blade. Do not let the saw teeth

Illus. 5-46. *For a right-hand mitre cut, turn the saw's arm to the right. Lock it at the desired angle.*

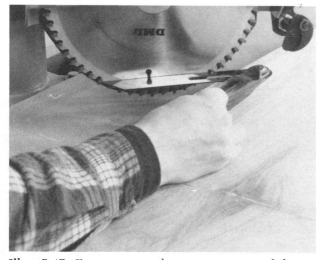

Illus. 5-47. *For exact angular settings, use a sliding T-bevel to set the angle.*

Illus. 5-48. *To copy the angle marked on the work, place a straightedge on the layout line and align the saw's arm with it.*

touch the blade of the sliding T-bevel. This could give you an incorrect adjustment.

A level or straightedge can also be used to copy the angle marked on the work. Place the straightedge on the layout line, and use your eyes to determine the arm angle. (See Illus. 5-48.) Pull the carriage towards you, and align the carriage with the straightedge. Clamp the arm in position after you have adjusted it correctly.

Now, return the carriage to the column. Then lower the blade until it is just above the table. Grab the carriage with one hand and turn on the motor with the other. While holding the car-

riage, slowly lower the blade into the table. If you have a front table that is higher than the back table, lower the blade enough to make a kerf in the front table. Then slowly pull the carriage through its entire stroke.

Before beginning to cut the work, take a practice cut in the waste area to ensure that the cut will be parallel to the layout line. (See Illus. 5-49.) Use the same methods for making the mitre cut as those used to make a crosscut.

To make a left-hand mitre, turn the saw's arm to the left. A left-hand mitre is best made with the table boards shifted and the fence in the rear position. This allows greater mitring capacity.

Set the mitre angle and pull the carriage through its stroke. If the blade leaves the table, set up a stop. (See Illus. 5-50.) An operating blade should never leave the table! That can lead to a dangerous situation. After cutting a kerf in the table and fence, cut the left-hand mitres.

Stops can be clamped to the table or fence to control the length of the parts. (See Illus. 5-51.) If stock tends to creep or move during a mitre cut, check the blade for a heeling condition. Clamp the work to the fence or table to eliminate any creeping during the mitre cut.

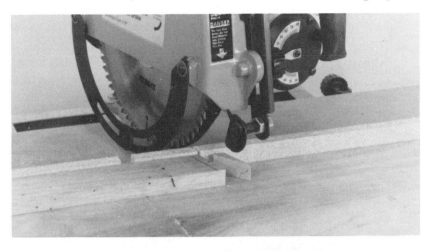

Illus. 5-49. *Make a practice cut in the waste area to be sure the setup is correct.*

Illus. 5-50. *The blade may leave the table on some left-hand mitre cuts. So, if possible, turn the work over and use the right mitre position. An arm clamp can be used to prevent the blade from leaving the table when it is cutting a left mitre.*

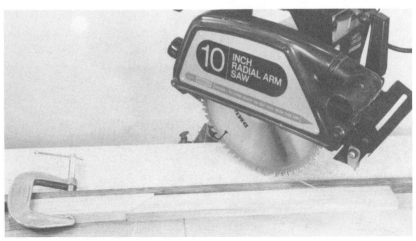

Illus. 5-51. *The stop clamped to the fence controls the length of the part. If stock tends to creep or move during the cut, check for blade heeling.*

End Mitres

End mitres are commonly used on pieces that edge-band plywood. They can also be found on some picture and clock frames. (See Illus. 5-52.) For end mitres, the arm remains locked in the 90-degree position, and the motor is tilted to the mitre angle. This angle is usually 45 degrees, but other angles may be set according to the job.

Illus. 5-52. *End mitres go from face to face on stock, and are made the same way as a crosscut.*

To tilt the motor, raise the blade about two inches above the table. Then release the clamp. (See Illus. 1-37.) Lift the locking pin and turn the motor to the desired angle. Use the protractor to determine the angle. (See Illus. 1-40.) For exact settings, use a sliding T-bevel to set the angle between the table and blade. You may have to lower the blade and carriage to make this adjustment.

Now, return the carriage to the column. Lower the blade until it is just above the table. Grab the carriage with one hand and turn on the motor with the other. While holding the carriage, slowly lower the blade into the table. If the front table is higher, lower the blade enough to cut a kerf in the front table. Now, pull the carriage and blade through the entire stroke. (See Illus. 1-41.) This will cut a kerf in the fence and table. Cut

end mitres using the same cutting techniques that are used for crosscutting. (See Illus. 5-53 and 5-54.)

Improving Face and End Mitres

Even after you have checked all adjustments on the radial arm saw and cut the mitres properly, the mitres may still fit poorly. The following factors can cause poorly made mitres. Eliminating them will improve the quality of the mitre cut.

1. A thin blade that flutters while cutting. This causes dips in the mitre. Use saw collars or a dampener to stiffen the blade, and check the arbor washers for distortion.

2. A stop that moves during the operation. This can cause one piece of the frame to be too long (or short). Banging stock against a stop while mitring can actually cause it to move.

3. The blade may not be perpendicular to the table. Check the motor clamp and lock to make sure that they are engaged correctly.

4. The blade is dull and tearing the wood. Replace the blade with a sharp one.

5. The object being framed is not square, thus affecting the fit of the mitre.

6. The framing stock does not have parallel edges.

7. Sawdust is trapped between the fence and the work. Clear the table frequently. Use a fence with a kerf. This will prevent sawdust from accumulating.

8. There is a heeling or alignment problem that is affecting the quality of the mitres.

Cutting Edge Mitres

An edge mitre is a rip cut made at an angle. To make this cut, the *yoke* must be turned 90 de-

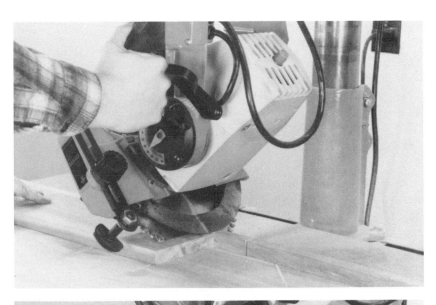

Illus. 5-53. *Hold the stock against the fence while the end mitre is being cut. An end-mitre cut is made like a crosscut.*

Illus. 5-54. *Return the carriage to the column after completing the end-mitre cut.*

Illus. 5-55. *Before making an edge mitre, check the blade for heeling.*

grees and the blade must be tilted to the desired mitre angle.

Before beginning, check the blade for heeling and adjust it if necessary. (See Illus. 5-55.) Replace the fence with a true, uncut piece of stock. Raise the blade about 1 inch above the front table. Release the yoke clamp and lift the yoke pin. Decide whether you wish to in-rip or out-rip, and turn the yoke 90 degrees (clockwise for in-rip, counterclockwise for out-rip). The yoke pin should drop into position. Give it a tap to make sure that it is seated correctly. The yoke clamp should now be locked.

Release the motor clamp and lift the locking pin. Turn the motor to the desired angle. (See Illus. 5-56.) Set the angle with the protractor

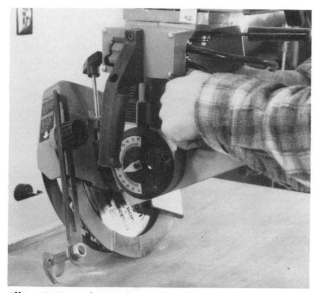

Illus. 5-56. *Release the motor clamp and pull the locking pin. Tilt the motor to the desired angle.*

scale, a triangle, or a sliding T-bevel. (See Illus. 5-57.) Cut a trough for the blade. Do this by lowering the turning blade until it touches the front table. Pull the blade through its stroke. The trough should be about ⅟₁₆ inch deep. Shut the saw off after the trough is cut.

Adjust the distance between the fence and blade to the desired width. Either measure this distance or use a piece of stock. If you measure, use a tooth on the blade that points towards the fence. If you use a piece of stock, move the carriage until the blade is lined up with the layout

line. (See Illus. 5-58.) Since this is done solely by sight, first make a practice cut in scrap stock.

Before making any cuts, lock the carriage and lower the guard to the work. Next, position the splitter and anti-kickback pawls. Clamp a cleat to the fence and use commercial hold-downs. The hold-downs will keep the stock from lifting during the cut.

Select a combination or rip blade with very little hook for this job. The less hook the blade has, the less chance that the stock will lift or kick back. Make the cut in the same way you make any other rip cut. (See Illus. 5-59.)

Special Mitre Setups

For some jobs, a special mitre setup may be needed. A shop-made mitring jig is commonly used on the radial arm saw for this purpose. (See Illus. 5-60.) When using a mitring jig, cut the left mitre first. (See Illus. 5-61.) Then move to the other side of the jig and cut the right mitre.

A stop can be clamped to the jig to control the length of the part. (See Illus. 5-62.) When using a jig such as this, use a carriage stop. The carriage stop controls the stroke of the carriage. This extra control makes any job safer, especially when repetitive mitre cuts are being made. Repetitive

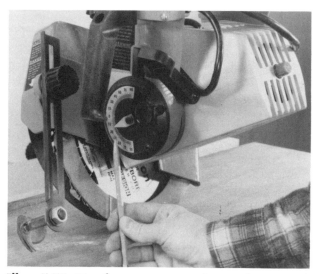

Illus. 5-57. *Use the protractor scale or a layout tool to set the desired angle. Clamp the motor in the desired position.*

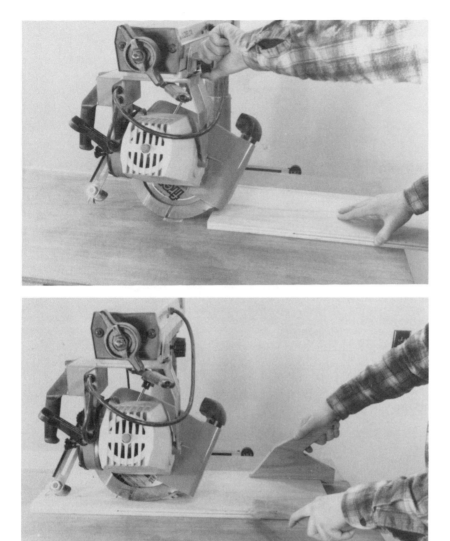

Illus. 5-58. *Move the carriage until the blade is aligned with the layout line on your workpiece. Lock the carriage to the arm.*

Illus. 5-59. *Position stock for an edge-mitre cut the same way you would position a piece that is to be ripped. The stock should clear the blade and lower guard before it is released.*

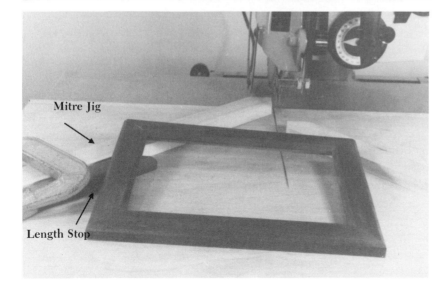

Illus. 5-60. *This mitring jig is clamped between the table boards. The saw's blade should be set perpendicular to the table, and the arm should be set at 0.*

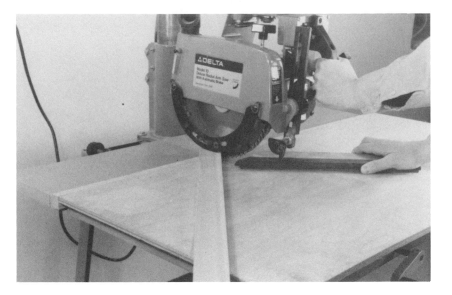

Illus. 5-61. *Make the left mitre cut first. Make this cut the same way you would make any crosscut.*

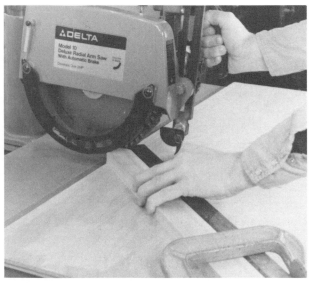

Illus. 5-62. *Make the right mitre cut. A stop block can be used to control the length of the part.*

You can buy manufactured mitre jigs that are similar to the shop-made one previously discussed. Both types of jig work on the principle of a 90-degree included angle. While the angle for each mitre cut may not be exactly 45 degrees, both angles add up to 90 degrees. As long as a mitre is cut on each side of the jig, the parts will fit at a perfect right angle.

Manufactured jigs also have a length gauge and a clamping device. (See Illus. 5-63.) The

Illus. 5-63. *This manufactured mitre jig holds stock at the desired angle for mitring. Make sure that the blade is positioned correctly. If it is not, you could cut the jig in half.*

cuts tend to be more dangerous. This is because it is difficult to maintain concentration or attention; the operator tends to daydream or think about the next task.

When using this jig, make the cut the same way you would make a crosscut. Pull the carriage towards you at a steady, even speed. Pulling the carriage too fast can cause tear-out or affect cutting accuracy.

clamping device holds the stock securely while the mitre is being cut. It also holds stock at any desired angle. This simplifies the cutting of compound mitres.

Cutting Chamfers and Bevels

Chamfers are inclined surfaces that go from the face of a piece to an edge or the end of the piece. Bevels are inclined surfaces that go from one face to another face on a piece of stock. (See Illus. 5-64.) Edge bevels are made with rip cuts. In fact, the cutting technique for an edge bevel, a chamfer, and a mitre is the same.

End chamfers and bevels are cut the same way as an end mitre. The angles may vary, but the technique is the same.

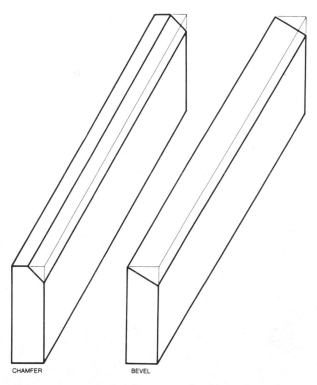

CHAMFER   BEVEL

Illus. 5-64. *A chamfer is an inclined surface that goes from a piece's face to an edge. A bevel goes from face to face.*

Using a Dado Head

A dado head is used to cut dadoes and rabbets. Dadoes are U-shaped channels that go through a piece of stock. Rabbets are L-shaped channels that go along the edge of a piece of stock.

There are actually three different types of dado head that can be used on the radial arm saw: the stack dado head, the adjustable wobble dado head and the adjustable V dado head. The stack dado head consists of two cutters and several chippers. (See Illus. 5-65.) (Cutters are similar to saw blades, but because of their tooth geometry are only used with the dado head.) The chippers go between the cutters and increase the width of the dado cut. Two cutters cut a ¼-inch-wide dado; each chipper increases the dado width by ¼, ⅛, or 1/16 inch. (See Illus. 5-66.)

A wobble dado head consists of a large center hub and a saw blade. (See Illus. 5-67 and 5-68.) As the center hub is turned, the saw blade is inclined. When the dado is mounted on the saw, the blade wobbles as it turns on the arbor. This causes it to cut a dado. The greater the incline of the blade, the wider the dado.

A twin-blade or adjustable V dado head has a large center hub with two 8-inch-diameter carbide-tipped saw blades mounted on it. As the hub is turned, the blades spread at one end only. This makes it look like the letter V. (See Illus. 5-69.) In each revolution of the dado head, the saw blades remove all the stock in their path, forming a dado. The adjustable V dado head is sold by DML and Sears. Sears calls its product the Excalibur™ dado head.

The adjustment collar at the center of the adjustable dado head indicates the approximate dado width. Mark the blade at its widest point to simplify setup. The adjustable V dado head also has a depth-of-cut scale to help you set dado depth. Each cutter on the adjustable V dado head is a 24-tooth carbide-tipped blade.

The hubs on adjustable V and wobble dado heads are quite thick and may not fit on the arbor of some radial arm saws. Be sure that your saw will accommodate the dado head before you buy it.

The quality of the dado cut by dado heads varies. Ask experienced woodworkers for their opinions before buying any dado head. Remember, even the best one will yield poor results on a radial arm saw with an alignment problem. Make sure that the blade is parallel to the fence and mitre slot.

Cutting Dadoes with a Dado Head

A dado head is usually used to cut dadoes. A dado is a rectangular channel in wood. To cut a dado with a dado head, first disconnect the power and remove the blade. (See Illus. 5-70.) Remove the blade from the arbor. (See Illus. 5-71.) Adjust the wobble or V dado head to the desired width. Then secure it to the arbor. (See Illus. 5-72.) When tightening the arbor nut, be careful not to change the setting on the adjustable wobble dado head.

If using a stack dado head, make sure that you select the correct combination of cutters and chippers. One or two cutters (blades) are always used. Chippers make up the rest of the combina-

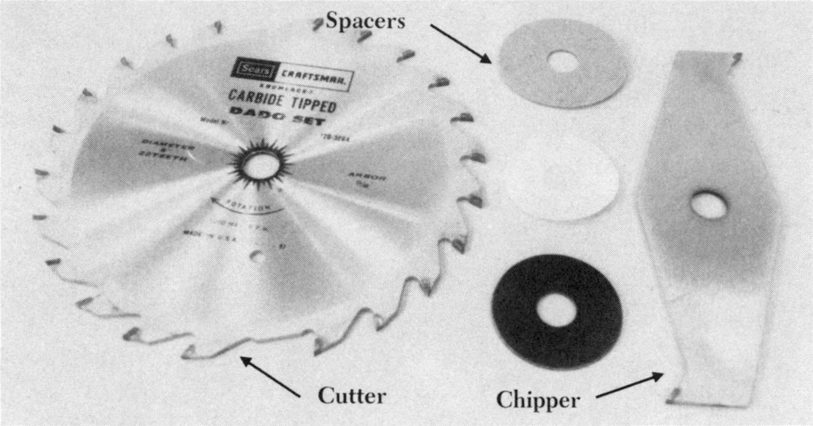

Illus. 5-65. *The stack dado head consists of two cutters and four to six chippers. The spacers are used for odd-sized dadoes. They go between the cutters and chippers.*

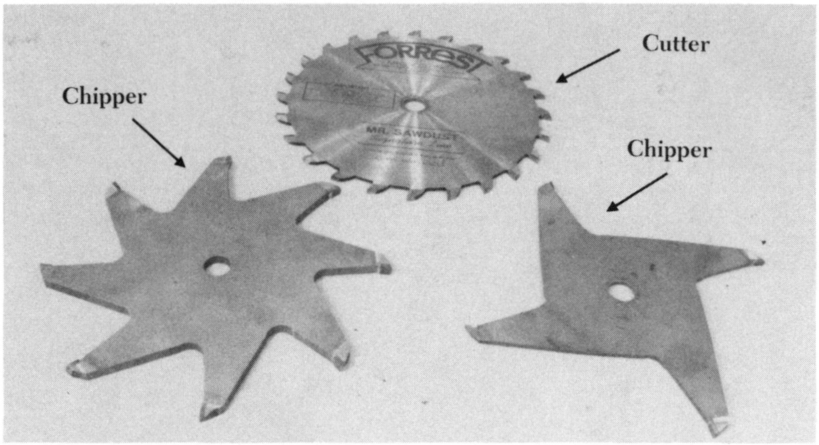

Illus. 5-66. *Some chippers have 4 to 8 cutting edges. The chipper shown here with 8 cutting edges is ¼ inch thick. The other chipper is ⅛ inch thick.*

Illus. 5-67. *A wobble dado head consists of a large center hub and a saw blade. As the hub is turned, the blade wobbles, causing it to cut a dado. Wobble dado heads vary in the number of cutters on the blade.*

Illus. 5-68. *Mark the high and low teeth with an etching pencil. This will make it easier to use a wobble dado head.*

Illus. 5-69. *A twin-blade or adjustable V dado head opens at one end only, and looks like the letter V when used.*

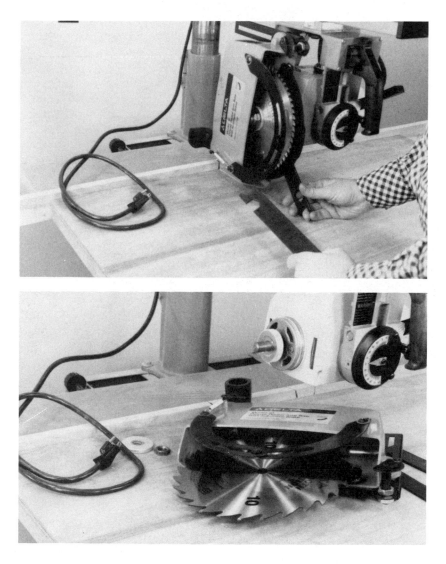

Illus. 5-70. *Disconnect the power and remove the blade. You will have to pivot the upper guard to gain access to the arbor nut.*

Illus. 5-71. *Remove the blade and guard assembly from the arbor.*

Illus. 5-72. *This adjustable V dado head has been set to the desired width and mounted on the arbor.*

tion. They are sandwiched between the cutters. A ½-inch dado head uses two ⅛-inch chippers.

You can use spacers to make minor adjustments in the dado-cutting size of the blades and chippers. (See Illus. 5-73.) Paper or plastic-laminate spacers can be placed between the cutters or chippers to increase dado width. To increase the dado width of a wobble dado head, turn or dial the washers.

Mount the dado head to the arbor carefully. The teeth closest to the table should point to-

Illus. 5-73. *When using a stack dado head, you can use spacers such as the ones shown here to make minor adjustments in the width of the dado.*

wards the fence. The chippers between the cutters should be staggered so that the head is balanced. (See Illus. 5-74.) The chippers closest to the cutters should rest or nestle in the gullets of the cutters. This keeps them from rocking.

Illus. 5-74. *Note how the chippers are staggered to give the head balance. The other cutter must be added before the arbor nut.*

The carbide-tipped blades used on some dado heads have two teeth missing. This allows for placement of the chippers. Placing the chippers in any other position could smash the carbide tips when the arbor nut is tightened.

Turn adjustable V dado heads to the desired width using the indicator at the hub. Mount the dado head to the arbor and secure the arbor nut. Try not to change the setting of the dado head when you tighten the arbor nut. Make sure that all the threads of the arbor nut are engaged with the threads of the arbor. (See Illus. 5-75). If not, do not use that dado head on the radial arm saw.

After replacing the guard, turn the dado head over by hand to make sure that it does not hit the guard. (See Illus. 5-76.) *All setup and preliminary checks should be made with the power disconnected.*

The species of wood, horsepower of the saw, and type of dado head being used will determine the appropriate dado depth. Generally, harder

Illus. 5-75. *Make sure that all the threads of the arbor nut are engaged with the arbor. Do not use the dado head if the nut is not fully engaged with the arbor.*

Illus. 5-76. *Turn the dado head over by hand before starting the cut, to make sure that it will not hit the guard. Do this with the power disconnected.*

woods like oak and beech require lighter cuts than softer woods like pine or basswood. As you become familiar with dado operations, you will know the limits of your radial arm saw and dado head. As a general rule, dado depth of ⅜ inch is suggested for each cut. If, however, a depth of ¾ inch is required, make the first cut ⅜ inch deep and the second cut ¾ inch deep.

Set the dado head's height and make a light cut on scrap. (See Illus. 5-77.) Make the cut and check the dado's width. Though the dado can be measured, the best way to verify its width is to check the fit between the dado and its mating part. (See Illus. 5-78.) There should be a snug but not a tight fit. Remember, when the glue is added, the fit will be a little tighter. Adjust the dado width if necessary, and set the dado depth.

The most accurate depth setting is made when the last movement of the blade is upwards. This ensures that there is no lash or slack between the gears in the elevating mechanism. Any slack in the gears will allow the blade height (and dado depth) to change.

Some dadoes can be cut with or against the grain. (See Illus. 5-79.) Not all dadoes are cut perpendicular to the stock. To make an angular dado, you will sometimes have to tilt the dado head and turn the arm. When setting up an angular cut, make sure that the dado head does not contact any metal object such as the column or table fasteners.

Tear-out around the dado is sometimes caused by a lack of set or clearance on the outside blades. This pinches the dado head, causing it to lift the wood fibres near the dado. A dull dado head will also tear the face of the work.

Pulling the carriage across the work too

Illus. 5-77. *Make a light cut on scrap to be sure the setup is correct.*

Illus. 5-78. *Check the fit between the dado and its mating part. This is the best measure of a proper fit.*

Illus. 5-79. *This dado cut is being made with the grain of the stock. The wheels on the Shophelper hold-down help control stock during the operation. Light cuts work best. The anti-kickback pawls ride on the work while the dado is being cut. This reduces the chance of a kickback.*

quickly can also cause tear-out. Vary your speed and compare the results. Cutting a deep dado can also cause tear-out. Raise the dado head and make a lighter cut. This will usually reduce tear-out.

It is worth the time it takes to change or move the fence when using a dado head. A new fence can eliminate tear-out on the end or edge of the work. The fence backs the work and keeps the end or edge of the work from tearing or splintering as the dado head begins its cut.

Another way to cope with tear-out is to cut dadoes in oversize stock, and then trim away the tear-out while cutting the piece to its finished size.

Some stack dado heads make the dado slightly deeper under the cutters. The cutters scribe the two sides of the dado, and the chippers remove the stock in between. The extra depth located at the cutters allows the stock cut by the chippers to break off evenly. Other stack dado heads cut dadoes of uniform depth.

Wobble dado heads cut a dado that sometimes has a concave (curving inward) or convex (bulging outward) bottom. This is a result of wobble in the blade. On wider dadoes, the dado head cuts deeper in the middle of the dado than on the edges. The larger the diameter of the wobble dado head, the more pronounced the effect.

If the dado is not visible, the slight irregularity will not affect gluing. If, however, you feel the dado should be trimmed, use a sharp chisel or router plane. Work carefully when trimming a dado. Make light cuts. Heavy cuts can leave the bottom of the dado more irregular than it was.

Keep the dado head sharp and free of pitch. A dull dado head produces poor results. Extra force is needed to cut with a dull dado head. This makes the dadoing operation unsafe.

Make sure that you use a dado head with carbide-tipped blades to cut dadoes in all sheet stock. Dado heads with tool-steel blades become dull rapidly in all materials except solid wood. Also, the glue and other additives in sheet stock are very hard. They take the edge off steel tools quickly.

The Freud® chip-limiting dado head is a stack dado head with a unique feature. Each tooth on the cutter has a metal ridge in front of it. (See Illus. 5-80.) This ridge limits the depth of cut or bite that each tooth takes. The chippers have a similar ridge or chip limiter.

When this dado head is used, feed speed is slower and tear-out is reduced. Since each tooth takes a smaller bite, there is less chance of kickback. This dado head is also a good selection for the radial arm saw since it will not climb the workpiece.

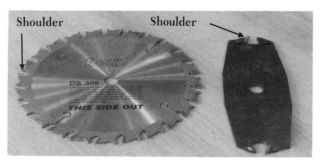

Illus. 5-80. *This chip-limiting dado head will not climb the workpiece and will reduce kickback and tear-out. The shoulder next to the carbide tip limits the cut.*

Cutting Dadoes in Plywood

Plywood is a difficult material to dado. This is because of its fibre core, which, in some cases, is so tough that it dulls the dado head. In other cases, the cross bands in the plywood break out and cause tear-out on the face of the plywood.

Plywood also varies in quality. Poor-quality plywood is not glued together as well as high-quality plywood. This results in tear-out on the face veneer as it breaks away from the bands beneath it. Poorer-quality plywood has cores that contain knots or twisted grain. When the dado head cuts through these defects, tear-out is more likely.

For best results when dadoing plywood, make sure that you have good control over the stock. (See Illus. 5-81.) Pull the carriage at a moderate speed. A rapid feed speed will encourage tear-out. In some cases, a light cut (about ¹⁄₁₆ inch deep) will establish shoulders on both sides of the dado. These shoulders then control the tear-our as a deeper cut is made. If problems persist, check the alignment of the saw blade. Heeling can cause tear-out.

Dado Quality

While dado quality varies from one dado head to another, poor-cutting dado heads can be used with good results. For example, if the dado looks rough from the front of the work, the dado can be stopped short of the edge.

Illus. 5-81. *This dado is being cut with a chip-limiting stack dado head. There is great control when the dado head is pulled into the plywood. There is no tear-out on this piece of plywood. When the saw is well aligned and the dado head is sharp, high-quality dadoes are made.*

Another way of achieving quality results with a poor-cutting dado head is to cut the dado narrower than its mating piece. (See Illus. 5-82.) The mating piece can then be rabbeted on both sides to fit the smaller dado. A dado head can be used for this operation, to eliminate tear-out. The shoulders of the rabbets hide the tear-out made by the dado head.

Cutting Rabbets with a Dado Head

Rabbets are L-shaped channels cut along an edge or end of stock. Rabbets (and dadoes) can be cut with a dado head or with a single blade. For one or two rabbets (or dadoes), it is probably faster to use a single blade, because it takes longer to set up a dado head than it takes to make the cut with a single blade. For cutting multiple parts, the dado head is much faster. The cut is made in one pass.

Rabbets cut on the end of stock with a dado head are cut much like single-blade rabbets. (See pages 96 and 97.) The saw arm is pulled across the work. Rabbets cut on the edge of stock require a special fence that is used with the dado head in the rip position.

To cut an end rabbet, mount the dado head onto the radial arm saw. The dado head should be as wide or slightly wider than the rabbet. *Make this setup with the power disconnected.*

Replace the guard and set the rabbet depth on scrap. Mount a stop on the fence. Position the stop so that it locates the rabbet correctly on the work. The work should be squarely against the fence and touching the stop.

Turn on the saw and pull the carriage through the work. (See Illus. 5-83.) Inspect the rabbet to ensure that it has been cut accurately and smoothly.

An angular end rabbet can be made in the same way. (See Illus. 5-84.) The only difference is that the motor is turned. When many of these rabbets must be cut, it is a good idea to use a carriage stop. This limits the travel of the arm and minimizes the chance of error during repetitive cuts.

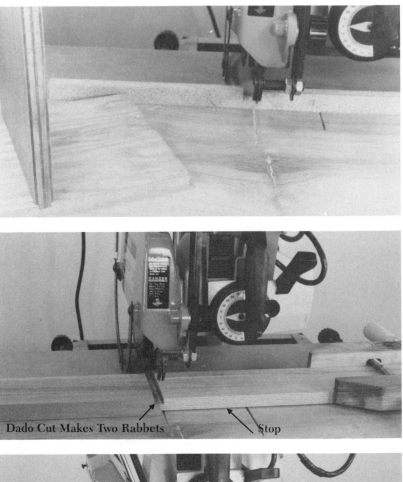

Illus. 5-82. *If tear-out is a problem, cut a rabbet on either side of the mating part. This will hide the tear-out.*

Illus. 5-83. *The stop positions the dado head to cut a rabbet in your workpiece. This cut is made just like a dado.*

Dado Cut Makes Two Rabbets   Stop

Illus. 5-84. *An angular end rabbet can be made by tilting the motor. The dado head cuts the work at an angle.*

Edge rabbets are set up differently. First, mount the dado head onto the arbor. The dado head should be about ¼ inch wider than the desired rabbet. Turn the yoke to the in-rip position, and install a new fence.

Next, mark the height of the rabbet on the fence above the table. Elevate the dado head above the fence and position it so that about one-third of the dado head is over the fence. Lock the carriage securely and position the guard horizontally. Turn the saw on and slowly lower the moving dado head into the fence.

Keep an eye on the mark scribed on the fence. When the dado head cuts the mark, begin elevating the head. (See Illus. 5-85.) Elevate it just enough to take any lash or slack out of the threads. Turn off the saw and allow the dado head to come to a complete stop.

Illus. 5-86. *Position the dado head relative to the fence. This allows the dado head to cut the desired rabbet.*

Illus. 5-85. *The fence can be rabbeted with a dado head. This allows the dado head to cut rabbets.*

Set the distance from the dado head to the fence to the desired rabbet size. (See Illus. 5-86.) Use a tooth on the outside cutter that points away from the fence. Position the hold-downs, guards, and anti-kickback devices and make a trial cut on scrap. Make any needed adjustments and begin rabbeting.

Use a push stick to control smaller pieces when rabbeting. Remember that hold-downs can make the operation much safer and the stock eas-

ier to control. (See Illus. 5-87.) If the saw slows down during the rabbeting operation, make a lighter cut. With practice, you will learn the correct depth of cut and feed rate for your radial arm saw.

The preferred way to cut rabbets on large pieces of sheet stock is to cut them on the edges of the stock with a dado head. Smaller pieces of sheet stock are usually rabbeted on their ends with a dado head.

Hardwood plywood may require a slower feed

Illus. 5-87. *Hold-downs make the rabbeting job safer and more accurate.*

rate than other materials. This is because the face veneers of hardwood plywood are very thin. These veneers tend to tear or break when cut at a high-feed rate. Remember, a carbide blade is better for sheet stock because the glue will dull tool-steel blades very quickly.

Single-Blade Rabbets

Single-blade rabbets (and dadoes) are sometimes called lazy dadoes. This implies that the operator is too lazy to set up a dado head. When you are cutting a few rabbets or dadoes, the single-blade method is the better method. When several dadoes and rabbets must be cut, set up a dado head. This reduces handling, labor, and setup time.

A single-blade rabbet is made in two cuts. To cut a rabbet, pivot the yoke to the rip position. Make the first cut on the face of the work. Control the depth of cut with the blade-elevation control. Set the blade to the full rabbet depth or slightly less. (See Illus. 5-88.) The distance from the fence to the far side of the blade determines the width of the rabbet on an edge of stock. Lock the carriage after making this adjustment. For some rabbets, this cut can be made at an angle.

Illus. 5-88. *The face cut for a rabbet on the edge of stock is made at full depth or slightly less.*

To make the second cut for the rabbet, turn the blade downwards into the horizontal position. Place an auxiliary table on the front table for this cut, and use a low fence. The safest way to make this cut is with a blade 8 inches in diameter or smaller. This allows you to use the sharper guard for this cut. Make sure that the blade does not touch the column. The shaper guard is an accessory made for the radial arm saw. It is available from the saw retailer or saw manufacturer. The shaper guard acts as a barrier when the blade is in the horizontal position.

Line the blade up with the other cut and lock it in position. Use a tooth that points towards the table for this setup. Install the shaper guard and make the cut. (See Illus. 5-89.)

Illus. 5-89. *The shaper guard is used for horizontal sawing. Make this cut in the same way as any rip cut.*

When an edge rabbet is being made, the edge of the stock rides along the fence. This is very similar to a rip cut. Use a push stick or hold-down to increase your control. End rabbets should be fed with a wide pusher block or mitre gauge. This keeps them from turning as the cut is made.

The end rabbet can also be made with a series of crosscuts. After making the first cut at the stop, move the work one saw blade away from the stop for another cut. (See Illus. 5-90 and 5-91.) Repeat these cuts until the rabbet is completed. (See Illus. 5-92.) Trim the rabbet with a chisel if necessary.

Illus. 5-90. *The face cut of this end rabbet was made with the work butted to the stop.*

Illus. 5-91. *Instead of turning the blade to the horizontal position, additional face cuts have been made.*

Illus. 5-92. *The rabbet is completed with a few additional face cuts. When cutting a few rabbets, this method is most efficient.*

Single-Blade Dadoes

To cut a dado across the face of your work, make a series of cuts. Line up your layout line with the blade and clamp a stop in position. Use a tooth that points towards the layout line. Make this cut on all pieces. (See Illus. 5-93.)

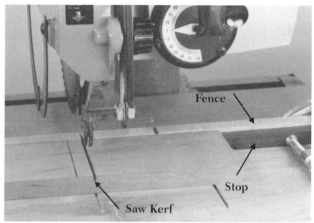

Illus. 5-93. *Position the stop so that the saw blade cuts the right shoulder of the dado. Make this cut on all parts.*

Now, move to the other layout line and position the blade. Use a tooth that points towards the layout line. Clamp a stop in position and make the cut. (See Illus. 5-94.)

Illus. 5-94. *Work from the second stop position, moving the piece further from the stop after each cut.*

Next, move the piece one saw-blade distance away from the stop and make another cut. (See Illus. 5-95.) Repeat the cuts until you reach the first kerf. Cut all the pieces before removing the stop. Avoid banging into the stop, as this may change your setup. Trim the dado with a chisel or router plane.

To cut a dado along the face of the work, position the yoke for ripping. Set the blade height to dado depth first, and then align the blade with

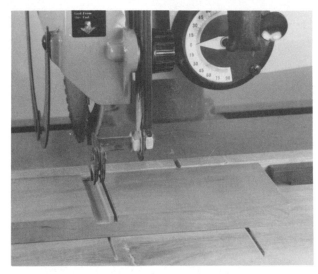

Illus. 5-95. *The dado progresses one saw kerf at a time.*

Illus. 5-96. *Position the blade for the shoulder of the dado closer to the fence. Make sure that the blade is in the waste area. Make the cut in the same way you make any other rip cut.*

the layout line closer to the fence. (See Illus. 5-96.) Use a tooth that points towards the fence. Lock the carriage to the arm after setting the blade distance from the fence.

Adjust the anti-kickback pawls and attach any available hold-downs or a cleat to the fence. This will provide greater control as you make the cut. Use a push stick to keep your hands clear of the blade. Make this cut on all pieces.

Release the carriage and align the blade with the other edge of the dado. Use a tooth that points away from the fence. Lock the carriage to the arm and make the cut on all parts. (See Illus. 5-97.)

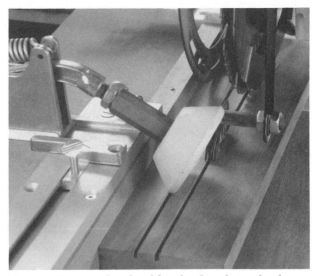

Illus. 5-97. *Cut the shoulder further from the fence after cutting all the parts at the first setting.*

Next, move the carriage one saw kerf closer to the fence, and make a cut. Make another cut on all the parts. Repeat these cuts until the dado has been completed. (See Illus. 5-98.)

The procedures for cutting single-blade rabbets and dadoes in sheet stock are similar to those used for solid stock. The difference is that the grain direction of sheet stock is not as important as the dimensions of the part. An end rabbet on a small piece of sheet stock would be made in the same way as an end rabbet on solid stock, but an end rabbet on a large, awkward piece of sheet stock would be treated as an edge rabbet in solid stock.

Illus. 5-98. *After a series of cuts, the dado is completed.*

Illus. 5-100. *Use the stock to position the stop for the length of the lapped area. Clamp the stop securely to the fence.*

Cutting Lap Joints

Lap joints are corner or cross joints where one piece laps over another. They are used for cabinet faceplates and for cross braces.

The lap joint is usually cut with a dado head. Adjust the dado-head depth to one-half stock thickness. (See Illus. 5-99.) For lap joints made on the end of stock, use the stock's width to locate a stop. (See Illus. 5-100.) Use a tooth that points away from the stop. Clamp the stop securely to the fence or table. The distance from the stop to the fence should equal the stock's width or slightly more. By allowing a little more distance, you will be able to sand the overlapping ends slightly after assembly to make a nice-looking corner.

Mark the pieces. One half will be cut on the good or exposed face of the stock. The other half will be cut on the back.

Butt the stock to the fence and stop just as if you were cutting an end rabbet. (See Illus. 5-101.) The stop shows the end of the cut. Pull

Illus. 5-99. *Begin the lap joint setup by setting the dado head depth to one-half the stock thickness.*

Illus. 5-101. *Mark all the parts. Remember, half of the parts will be cut on the good or exposed side of the stock, the other half on the bad side. Then butt the stock to the stop and make the first cut. Hold the stock securely against the fence.*

the carriage through the work and return it to the column. Now, move the stock just enough to make another cut. (See Illus. 5-102.) Continue this practice until the cut is completed. (See Illus. 5-103.)

Note: If the pieces tear out at the back of the stock when they are cut, back them up with a new fence. The new fence will control tear-out. Careful layout and setup will yield a good-fitting lap joint. (See Illus. 5-104.)

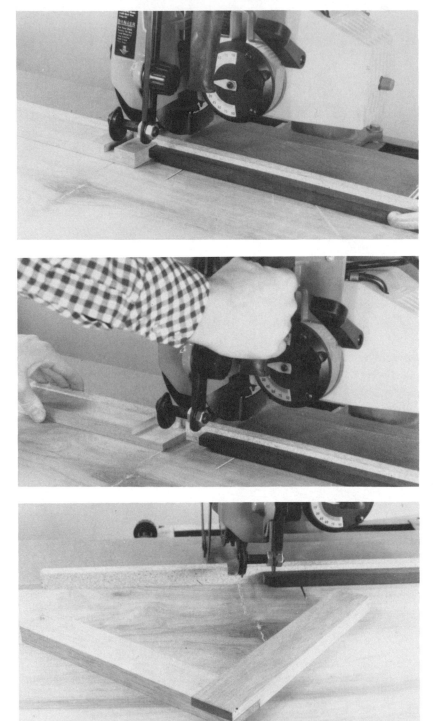

Illus. 5-102. *Move the stock away from the stop just far enough to make another cut.*

Illus. 5-103. *Continue moving the piece until the cut is complete. Do not move the stop until all the parts have been cut.*

Illus. 5-104. *Careful layout and setup will yield a good-fitting lap joint. Make a practice cut in scrap to be sure of the setup.*

When cutting a cross-lap joint, you must use two stops. This is because the stops are not on the end of the piece. Set the first stop so that the dado head cuts the shoulder nearer to the stop. (See Illus. 5-105.) Remember, this stop will be lined up with the right side of the dado head (the side closer to the stop). Butt the work against the fence and stop. Make the first cut and check the setup. (See Illus. 5-106.) Make this cut on all parts and remove the stop.

Position the second stop on the left of the layout line. Use the left side of the dado head. (See Illus. 5-107.) Position the work and make the cuts. (See Illus. 5-108.) Both ends of the cross-lap

Illus. 5-105. *Position the stop so that the dado head cuts the shoulder nearer to the stop.*

Illus. 5-106. *Make the first cut with the stock butted against the stop. Cut all parts at this setting.*

Illus. 5-107. *Position the stop to cut the shoulder further from the stop. Make this cut on all parts.*

Illus. 5-108. *Several identical cross-lap joints can be produced accurately with this method.*

joint are now cut. If more stock remains, continue cutting until it is gone. Several identical cross-lap joints can be produced accurately with this method. (See Illus. 5-108.)

When making cross-lap joints, make sure that the stock is of uniform thickness and width. Wide pieces will need trimming, and narrow pieces will fit poorly.

Uniform stock thickness is also important when you are making any lap joint. Thick or thin stock will produce a shoulder at the joint. This spoils the appearance of the work and wastes material.

Remember to use an arm stop or clamp if multiple parts are being cut. This reduces the chance of error and accident. It saves time, also, since the pull stroke will only be as long as necessary.

Sanding Operations

The radial arm saw is quite versatile as a sanding machine. (Sanding is smoothing the wood by grinding it with an abrasive.) It is capable of disc-sanding and spindle-sanding. Each of these operations requires a different setup. The specifics of each are discussed below.

Whenever you use the radial arm saw for sanding operations, wear a dust mask and use a dust collector. The dust of some woods is capable of causing bronchial problems and cancer. Using dust masks and other dust-collection systems can make the sanding operation much safer.

Regardless of the type of sanding operation being set up, make sure that the attachments are secured properly and that all adjustments have been properly made before you begin sanding. *Make all adjustments and setups with the power disconnected.*

Disc-Sanding

Mount the sanding disc on the arbor in the same way as a blade. (See Illus. 5-109 and 5-110.) Then turn the yoke so that the disc faces forward. A special shop-made sanding table is used to support the work while it is being sanded. (See Illus. 5-111.) Clamp the sanding table to the table of the radial arm saw. Adjust the sanding table so that it is about ⅛ inch from the disc. Make sure that the saw's arm and carriage are locked securely before you begin sanding.

All sanding is done against disc rotation. If sanding an outside curve, turn on the power and feed the work into the disc. Take a light cut and keep the work moving. This will keep the abrasive from burning the wood. Always work on the half of the disc that is moving downwards towards the table. (See Illus. 5-112.) If you work on the half of the disc moving upwards, the disc will lift the work.

The most common error made when disc-sanding is to load or burn the disc with wood particles. A loaded disc gets hot and will become burned quickly. A burned disc will not cut. A stick-type abrasive cleaner will keep the disc from loading.

Although burning is most often caused by a loaded disc, it can also be caused in part by using too fine an abrasive for the job or not moving the part as it is sanded. Keeping the part stationary while sanding causes heat to build up on both the disc and the wood. Move the wood and use the

Illus. 5-109. *Remove the guard and saw blade to use the radial arm saw for disc-sanding. Do this with the power disconnected.*

Illus. 5-110. *Mount the sanding disc in the same way as you would a saw blade, except that the guard is not used.*

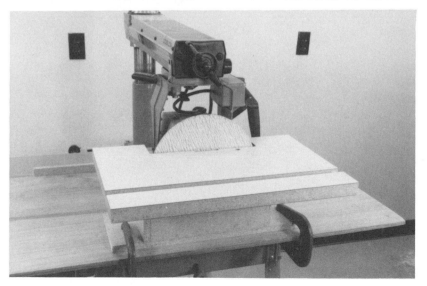

Illus. 5-111. *A special sanding table should be made for disc-sanding. This table should be clamped to the radial-arm-saw table.*

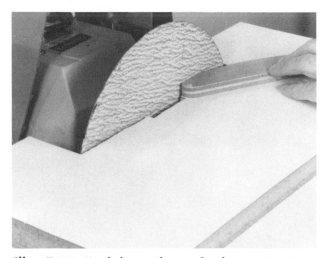

Illus. 5-112. *Feed the work into the disc against its rotation. Keep the work moving, to prevent the abrasive from burning the wood. Always work on the downward side of the disc. This keeps the stock positioned and you in control of the job.*

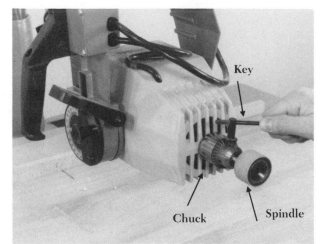

Illus. 5-113. *A chuck has been mounted onto the auxiliary arbor. This chuck can hold various sanding attachments. A small spindle has been checked for spindle-sanding.*

entire downwards-moving half of the disc. Remember, heat will build up faster at the outer edge of the disc. This is because the disc turns faster at the outer edge.

Because a sanding disc does not have teeth, some woodworkers feel that it is not as dangerous as a saw blade. This is inaccurate. A sanding disc is full of abrasive particles, which are similar to small blade teeth. These teeth take smaller bites, but cut just the same. Keep your hands clear of the disc and table. If your finger becomes pinched between the disc and sanding table, a serious injury can occur.

Spindle-Sanding

When internal curves or irregular edges must be sanded, spindle-sanding works better than disc-sanding. Spindles come in diameters that range from about ½ to 3 inches. They vary in length from 1 to 3 inches.

Sanding spindles can be mounted onto the blade arbor, an auxiliary arbor, or a chuck attached to the blade or auxiliary arbor. (See Illus. 5-113 and 5-114.) Where you will mount the sanding spindle depends on the type of radial arm saw and the type of sanding spindle. For best results, make an auxiliary table. (See Illus. 5-115.) This

Illus. 5-114. *This abrasive spindle is threaded to mount directly to the auxiliary arbor.*

allows you to move the spindle up and down to use all of the abrasives.

To sand bevels or chamfers, tilt the spindle. Make sure all locks are secure after you have adjusted the spindle. Use relatively coarse abrasives (40- to 80-grit) when spindle-sanding, and use an abrasive cleaner to keep the abrasives from loading and burning. (See Illus. 5-116.)

The spindle may be used in any position, depending on the work. In some cases, it is easier to put the spindle in the horizontal position and sand the work freehand. Exercise caution when freehand-sanding. Keep your fingers clear of the abrasives at all times. Abrasives can tear your skin very quickly. Be sure to wear a dust mask and use a dust collector for all sanding operations.

Illus. 5-115. *A special table can be made to make spindle-sanding easier.*

Illus. 5-116. *Keep the work moving and use a relatively coarse abrasive. This will keep the work from burning.*

Chapter 6

ADJUSTING THE RADIAL ARM SAW

Adjustment techniques can be the most challenging and vexing part of radial-arm-saw maintenance. Adjustment problems can be minimized, however, if you use the saw correctly. Many people do not. Some operators jerk the carriage through the work with no concern for the tool. The blade climbs the work and throws the saw out of alignment. Also, some carpenters carry their saws from job to job; they pay no attention to how the saw is loaded or transported. These are a few examples of how mistreatment can throw the radial arm saw out of alignment.

Blade selection can also affect how the saw performs. A saw blade with a great deal of hook can climb when used to make crosscuts and rip cuts. The blade itself may cause alignment problems.

Sometimes, even when the saw is adjusted properly, a thin blade will deflect during the cut. Though this may suggest an adjustment problem, deflection will cease when a more massive blade or a saw collar is used. It is good practice to determine what is causing the problem before undertaking major adjustment of your saw.

The following adjustment checks are general steps that can be used for all radial arm saws. They will help you diagnose and make the specific adjustments explained by the manufacturer's or owner's manual. Read all of the steps through before beginning. *Work carefully, and with the power disconnected.* Make any test cuts

with all the stops and clamps engaged. When making adjustments, however, release the clamps to allow movement or readjustment.

1. *The table should be parallel to the arm.* Begin by removing the blade and guards. Turn the arbor to the vertical position. (See Illus. 6-1.) Lower the arbor so that it is about 1/16 inch away from the table. Pull the carriage so that the arbor is over the front table.

Look at the arbor and table; observe any deviation of space between them. Now, swing the arm to various positions while pulling the car-

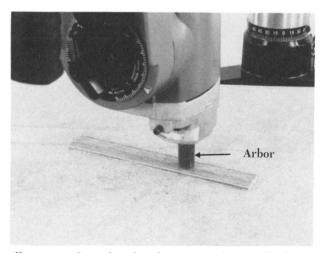

Illus. 6-1. *The arbor has been turned towards the table. This check will determine if the table is parallel to the arm. A shim is used as a feeler gauge.*

riage through its stroke. Note any deviation of space between the table and arbor. (See Illus. 6-2.) If there is deviation, the table is not parallel to the arm. Check the table to see if it is true. Use a straightedge to check for warp. (See Illus. 6-3.)

If the table is warped, most saws provide some mechanism for adjustment. Usually, you can raise or lower the table in the middle by tighten-

ing or loosening a threaded device. (See Illus. 6-4.) Straighten the table and then check the table with the arbor again.

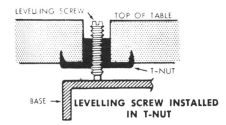

Illus. 6-4. *Raise or lower the levelling screw in the center of the table to remove any table warp.*

If deviation still exists, remove the table. Then use the arbor to true-up the table brackets. (See Illus. 6-5–6-7.) A spacer can be used between the arbor and the brackets. This will allow you to move the brackets without having to raise the arbor. When the brackets are in the same plane, replace the table.

2. *The table edge should be perpendicular to blade travel.* Turn the arbor to the horizontal position and mount a blade to it. Lock the column perpendicular to the table and move it near the blade. Place a square next to the blade. Slowly pull the carriage through its stroke.

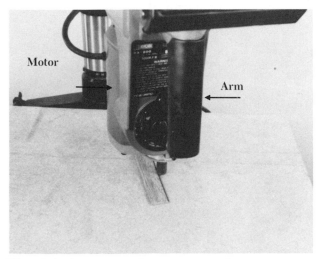

Illus. 6-2. *By moving the carriage and arm, you can determine if the table is parallel to the arm at different positions. This position suggests that the table is not parallel to the arm.*

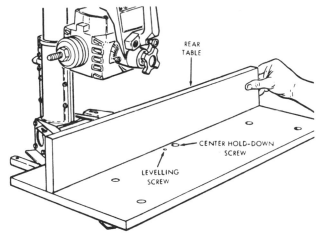

Illus. 6-3. *Use a straightedge to check for table warp. (Drawing courtesy of Sears, Roebuck, & Co.)*

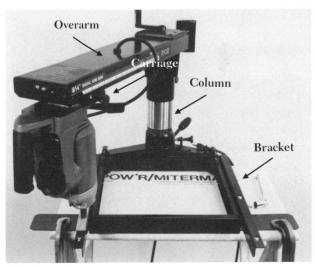

Illus. 6-5. *If the table is still not parallel to the arm, remove the table and check the brackets.*

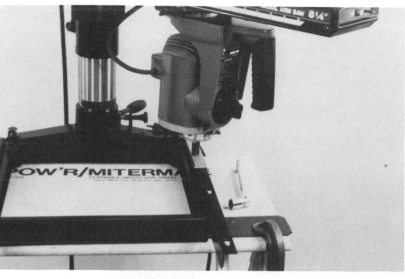

Illus. 6-6. *The brackets must be parallel to the arm. Check both ends of the table brackets to ensure they are parallel to the arm.*

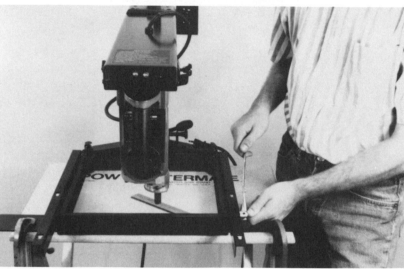

Illus. 6-7. *Use a wrench to secure the brackets at the desired setting.*

Watch the blade and the square. The blade and the square should remain parallel throughout the saw's stroke. (See Illus. 6-8.) If the two are not parallel, loosen the table and move it slightly. When the square and blade remain parallel through the stroke, tighten the table.

Some machines also have columns that can be adjusted. If using this method, you will move the arm instead of the table. In most cases, it is easier to shift the table. Through practice, you will be able to determine which is the better method to use on your saw.

Illus. 6-8. *When you replace the table, make sure that the front edge of the table is perpendicular to the blade's path.*

3. *The blade should be perpendicular to the table.* Set a try square on the front table and move it against the blade. Make sure that the

bevel pin or latch is engaged. Also, secure the lock knob or clamp.

The blade part of the square should be up against the body of the blade. (See Illus. 6-9.) Do not let the tooth set affect your reading. If the blade is not perpendicular to the table, adjustment is necessary.

Illus. 6-9. *Check the blade to be sure that it is perpendicular or square with the table. If it is not, the motor must be adjusted. This adjustment is usually made near the bevel latch and lock knob.*

Most saws are adjusted adjacent to the bevel latch and lock knob. The adjusting screws are found within the bevel-angle indicator. On some saws, the angle-indicator plate must be removed for access to the adjusting screws.

This procedure requires that you loosen the bevel clamp or lock knob. The bevel pin or latch remains engaged. Loosen the setscrews slightly. There may be 2, 3, or 4 setscrews, depending on the brand of machine.

Next, turn the motor so that the blade is perpendicular to the table; then tighten the setscrews. Check the square frequently while tightening the setscrews. As the screws are tightened, the motor and blade may shift slightly. Tighten the screws uniformly. Do not tighten one screw completely. Tighten all screws gradually.

4. *The blade should not heel.* Heeling is a condition where the rear of the blade does not follow

the same path as the front of the blade. (See Illus. 6-10.) Heeling can be observed when you are crosscutting. As the rear half of the blade enters the work, the kerf becomes wider. This can also cause tear-out.

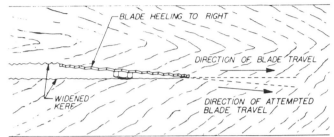

Illus. 6-10. *Heeling occurs when the front and back of the blade are not in the same plane. This can cause grain tear-out or the blade to bind when it is used to cut. (Drawing courtesy of Northfield Foundry and Machine Co.)*

When you are making rip cuts, heeling can push the board towards or away from the fence. This can cause burning in the kerf or kickbacks.

Check for heeling by placing a square against the fence and across the blade. (See Illus. 6-11.) Any space between the square and the blade indicates a heeling condition.

Illus. 6-11. *Place a square against the fence and along the blade at a 40- to 60-degree angle. The square should be in contact with the entire blade. If it is not, an adjustment must be made at the carriage or rear motor pivot.*

Heeling is eliminated on some machines by adjusting the carriage. On other machines, the rear motor mount is moved in the yoke. When the square butts to the blade, heeling should be eliminated.

5. *The splitter should be aligned with the saw kerf.* For accurate and safe rip cuts, the splitter must be in the same plane as the blade. Most manuals recommend that you align the splitter with the blade by sight. It can also be done with a piece of stock, as follows.

Clamp a scrap of plywood about 6 to 10 inches wide to the table. Make a crosscut through about 8 inches. Return the carriage to the column and shut off the saw. Disconnect the power and pull the carriage back until the blade is in the kerf. Now, drop the splitter and adjust it so that it is centered in the kerf. (See Illus. 6-12.)

Illus. 6-12. *Move the blade back into the cut and center the splitter in the kerf. Do this with the power disconnected.*

Compensating for Wear

Most machines have adjustments that allow you to compensate for wear in the parts. The most common places wear occurs are in the column,

carriage and yoke, which become loose. Most machines have clamps on the back side of the column that can be used to tighten the column. It is possible to tighten these fasteners so much that the column will not move. This should be avoided. Be careful when tightening the column clamps. (See Illus. 6-13.)

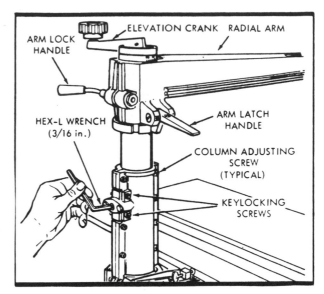

Illus. 6-13. *When tightening the clamps on the back of the column, be careful. It is possible to over-tighten the column. The column must be loose enough to move. (Drawing courtesy of Sears, Roebuck, & Co.)*

A loose carriage can be tightened by adjusting the carriage roller bearings. Two of the bearings on the carriage have an eccentric center hole. This allows them to be tightened against the arm. This tightens the carriage.

If the carriage is tight, clean the tracks within the arm. (See Illus. 6-14.) A cloth dampened with mineral spirits works well.

After being cycled numerous times, the clamp mechanism on the yoke will begin to wear, and the loose yoke will not pull up snugly against the carriage. Access for tightening the yoke is usually provided immediately under the yoke clamp. Refer to the manufacturer's instructions for specifics.

Getting the Best Cut

In working with the radial arm saw, I have observed that shaping, dadoing, and other more advanced cuts are usually best made when the work is fed into a stationary blade. Experience will suggest the best and safest cutting approach.

When working with the blade in a stationary position, make sure that it remains stationary. Some clamps and locks cannot be tightened securely enough by hand. In some cases, the hand knob may be replaced with a hex-head bolt.

Regardless of whether the blade remains stationary or not, there are other problems that can affect the cut. They include:

1. *Workpiece irregularities.* The edge of the work will not butt to the fence or rest on the table in a true plane.

2. *Chips or sawdust.* Sawdust or chips of wood get between the work and fence or table. This can affect the accuracy or the quality of the cut.

3. *Stock is not held securely.* The workpiece moves during an angular crosscut. This affects the quality and accuracy of the cut. The stock can also move when you in- or out-rip, also causing problems with the accuracy and quality of the cuts. Use commercial hold-downs or featherboards in these situations to help prevent the workpiece from moving.

4. *Blade problems.* A dull blade can usually affect the quality and accuracy of the cut. Drag your thumbnail across the carbide tip of a blade to see if it is sharp. (See Illus. 6-15.) A sharp tip will raise a chip on your nail. One indication that tool-steel blades are dull is a small rounded area that appears where the edges of the teeth come together.

A blade with too many teeth may cause burning in some rip and crosscuts, and a blade with too few teeth or too much hook can cause tearout. A blade that flutters can make an uneven cut. Sometimes a saw collar will prevent the blade from fluttering.

While working with the saw, you may discover other causes for a poor cut. The more you work with your saw, the more obvious any decrease or increase in the quality of the cut will be. The ability to perceive these differences is almost as satisfying as a quality cut.

Illus. 6-14. *Keep the tracks clean to ensure smooth carriage movement. Chips can accumulate on the tracks or bearings if oil is used as a lubricant.*

Illus. 6-15. *Drag your thumbnail across the carbide tip of a blade to see if it is sharp. A sharp tip will raise a chip on your nail. A dull tip will slide across your nail.*

Minimizing Tear-Out Problems

One annoying problem that operators will come across when sawing is grain tear-out. Tear-out can occur on the face or back of the work, or on the edge next to the fence. If a wrong blade or dull blade is used, tear-out is sure to occur. Heeling will usually cause tear-out on the upper face of the work. A rip blade or a blade with a great deal of hook or a blade that is pulled into the wood too quickly can also cause tear-out. A moderate cutting speed will reduce tear-out.

One of the best ways of eliminating tear-out on the edge of the stock next to the fence is by installing an uncut fence or moving the present one over to an uncut area. The uncut fence supports the work everywhere except the kerf. This controls tear-out on the edge against the fence.

Tear-out through the top and bottom of the stock can be controlled by taping or scoring the stock. (Scoring is making a knife cut through the piece on the cutting line.) Generally, the cause of tear-out on the bottom face is a lack of support for the work; that is, the table has been cut away, and the wood fibres have no support. This makes it easy for the fibres to tear.

Tape applied over the area to be cut holds the fibres in place. The blade cuts through the tape, and the tape holds the fibres down on both sides of the kerf.

Scoring the layout line with a utility knife will cause the wood fibres to break evenly at the line. A sharp utility knife must be used. Score the wood to a depth of 1/16 inch or greater. Scribe both faces and edges to completely control tear-out.

Chapter 7

PROJECTS

This project chapter is last for good reason. You must read, understand, and digest the material in the first six chapters before you can build these projects. If you begin a project without a full understanding of radial-arm-saw operations, you could waste material or incur an injury.

Plan the projects carefully. Read the related sections in the book before beginning any operation.

Procedures for Building Projects

When building any project, pay attention to the following procedures. These procedures will help you do a better job with fewer mistakes.

1. *Study the drawings carefully.* Check the dimensions or scale on the project drawings to be sure that all the parts will be cut and machined correctly. Make allowances for joints or for parts that will be trimmed. Remember, some jigs have dimensions suited for a particular saw. These dimensions may have to be changed to fit your saw.

2. *Develop auxiliary sketches when needed.* When you have modified the drawings or an assembly is complex, make an auxiliary sketch. Keep this sketch next to the radial arm saw. It will help you determine how the parts must be cut. Extra sketches will make radial-arm setups quicker and more accurate.

3. *Develop a bill of materials.* A bill of materials is a list of all the parts needed to build the project. The list includes the part's dimensions (thickness, width, and length). The bill of materials makes stock selection easier. It also helps you to set stops on the radial arm saw when cutting parts to length.

4. *Write a plan of procedure.* The plan of procedure is a list of steps one should follow to build the project. The plan is an orderly list or series of operations. For example, a drawer opening would be made before a drawer front is cut to exact size.

5. *Think before making any cuts.* Plan your cutting, to reduce the chance of error. When cutting parts, cut the longest parts first. Any parts cut too short can then be used for shorter parts on the bill of materials.

Before making a cut in the work, test the setup on scrap. Make sure that the setup is correct before beginning. Mark complex cuts.

When several operations are being performed on a number of parts, mark the control edge of each part. This is the edge of the part that always rides against (or away from) the fence. These marks will minimize the chance that you will accidentally reverse the parts after performing a few operations. They are important on parts such as moulding, picture-framing, and cabinet sides.

6. *Check the fit of all parts before assembling them.* Fit the parts together dry before gluing them. Parts that fit tightly or loosely can cause

problems. Parts that fit tightly will be impossible to assemble when glue is applied. Glue will cause both parts to swell and require that they be forced together. Sometimes the glue sets before the parts are positioned correctly. This brings the entire assembly to a halt.

Parts that fit loosely will have a weak glue joint. These parts can also cause alignment problems, since the mating parts can shift. Remember, it is easier to make minor adjustments and trim the parts or add a shim to them when there is no glue on the parts.

7. *Plan ahead for finishing.* Sand all the internal surfaces before assembling a box or cabinet. These surfaces may be difficult or impossible to sand after assembly. It may also be easier to apply a stain and finish to these surfaces before assembly.

Watch for glue smears on the wood. They can make the stain and finish appear blemished. Circle glue smears with chalk when you notice them. This will help you eliminate them during surface preparation. Scrape or sand away these smears before applying a stain or finish.

8. *Properly maintain your radial arm.* A poorly maintained radial arm saw seldom cuts accurately. It is difficult to get good cuts from a saw that is not maintained correctly. It is well worth the extra time involved to readjust a radial arm saw. Using a saw that is out of alignment can damage the blade and will yield poor work.

Jig-building Techniques

Most jigs designed to be used on a radial arm saw are controlled by the table or the fence when the arm, carriage, or jig is moved. (See Illus. 7-1.) When making a jig for your radial arm saw, select stock carefully. Sheet stock is a good material for jig construction because it resists warping, swelling, and wear. Make the cleats on your radial-

Illus. 7-1. *This spindle-sanding jig is controlled by the table. Clamps hold it securely in position. Movement of the arm or carriage positions the spindle. This jig is a worthwhile accessory for your radial arm saw.*

arm-saw jigs out of a dense hardwood. This will keep the control surfaces from wearing, and will prevent the cleat from being crushed when it is clamped between the table boards.

Always consider safety when designing a jig for the radial arm saw. Many times the saw owner builds the jig carelessly because it is not regarded as an important part of the operation. A well made jig will be an accurate device that can be used for many different operations. A poorly made jig may be dangerous, yield poor results, and be used only once.

A safe jig is planned carefully. It is built as an accessory for the radial arm saw. It fits correctly and can be mounted or installed easily.

When building jigs for your radial arm saw, make sure you know the blade's path and how you can keep clear of the path..

Vision is also important. You have to be able to see the work and the blade. You can use clear plastic on some jigs as a barrier between you and the work or blade. Clear plastic limits contact with the blade, but does not limit vision.

Basic Jigs and Accessories

The first items you should make for your radial arm saw are safety jigs and accessories. These include push sticks, push blocks, featherboards, auxiliary front tables, and extra fences, all of which have been examined in Chapter 1.

Push Sticks

Push sticks should be made as soon as you begin working with your saw. Cut the push sticks out with a sabre, scroll, or band saw using the patterns in Illus. 7-2–7-5. Then make a spindle-sanding attachment, shown in Illus. 7-6, to smooth the edges of the push stick. Use a router to round over the edges. (See Illus. 7-7.) A round edge is not as likely to cut you in the event of a kickback.

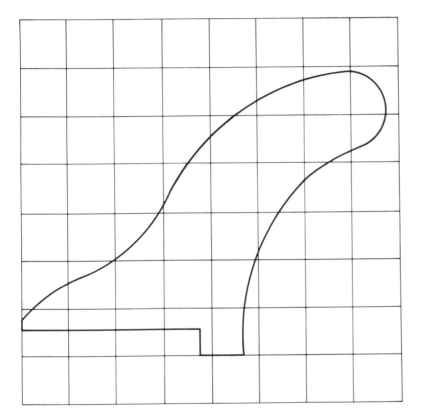

Illus. 7-2. *Use this pattern to make push sticks to be used on your radial arm saw. Modify it to suit your needs, but avoid sharp corners and edges. This pattern and the pattern for Illus. 7-3 are on a 1-inch grid that has been reduced.*

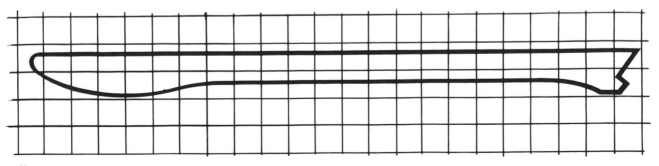

Illus. 7-3.

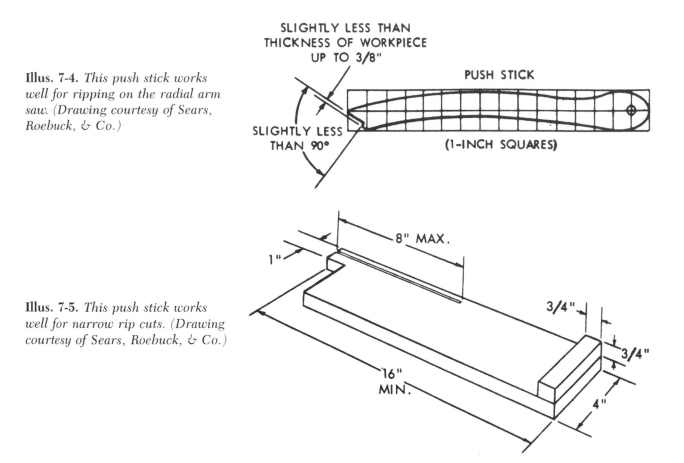

Illus. 7-4. *This push stick works well for ripping on the radial arm saw. (Drawing courtesy of Sears, Roebuck, & Co.)*

SLIGHTLY LESS THAN THICKNESS OF WORKPIECE UP TO 3/8"

PUSH STICK

SLIGHTLY LESS THAN 90°

(1-INCH SQUARES)

Illus. 7-5. *This push stick works well for narrow rip cuts. (Drawing courtesy of Sears, Roebuck, & Co.)*

8" MAX.

1"

3/4"

3/4"

16" MIN.

4"

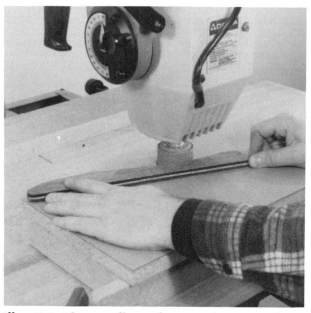

Illus. 7-6. *This spindle-sanding attachment can be used to smooth the handle of your push sticks.*

Illus. 7-7. *Use a router and roundover bit to round the edges of your push stick. They will be more comfortable and less likely to cut your hand.*

Drill a hole in the push sticks so that they can be hung near the saw. Make some hooks that can be mounted on the radial arm saw. These hooks ensure that a push stick will be where it is needed at all times.

Featherboard

A featherboard helps control stock when you are making rip cuts or shaping on the radial arm saw. Make several featherboards while the saw is set up. Keep them handy for future use.

To make a featherboard, select a piece of stock about ¾ inch thick, 4 inches wide and 36 inches long. Use two spacer sticks and the fence to space the kerfs evenly. One stick should be as thick as the desired "feathers," and the other should be as thick as one feather and a saw kerf.

Cut the ends of the workpiece at a 30- to 45-degree angle before making any kerf cuts. Mark the feather length (about 4½ inches) with a pencil. Position the blade for in-ripping, cut a trough, and install an uncut fence.

Set the distance between the blade and fence with the thinner stick. (See Illus. 7-8.) Lock the carriage in position. Turn on the saw and make the first cut. (See Illus. 7-9.) When the blade reaches the layout line, shut off the saw and let the blade coast to a stop. Do not move the workpiece. Make the same cut on the other end.

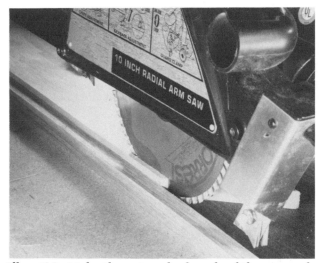

Illus. 7-9. *Make the cut on both ends of the piece of stock. Shut off the saw when the blade reaches the layout line.*

With the blade still in the work, unlock the carriage and insert the thicker stick between the fence and the work. (See Illus. 7-10.) Lock the carriage in this position. Pull the work off the blade and move it over to the fence. Turn on the saw and make the second cut. (See Illus. 7-11.) Let the blade coast to a stop when it reaches the layout line. Make the same cut on the other end of the work. (See Illus. 7-12.) Continue this process until you reach the other edge.

Illus. 7-8. *Use the thinner stick to adjust the distance from the fence to the blade.*

Illus. 7-10. *Move the blade over by inserting the thicker stick between the blade and fence. The work should remain in contact with the blade. Lock the carriage at this setting.*

Illus. 7-11. *Make the second cut. Let the blade coast to a stop when it reaches the layout line. Then make the same cut on the other end of the work.*

Illus. 7-13. *If the last feather is too wide or narrow, saw along the entire edge to eliminate it.*

Illus. 7-12. *Continue making the cuts. Always stop at the layout line and allow the blade to come to a complete stop.*

The last feather may be wider or narrower than the others. (See Illus. 7-13.) You can also eliminate it by simply cutting along the entire edge, thus sawing it off. Sand the featherboard lightly, and it will be ready for use.

Cut the stock into two equal pieces and you will have two featherboards.

Fences

Fences are also an important accessory that you can easily make. You should always have several extra fences on hand so that they will be available when you need them.

Most new radial arm saws come equipped with a particleboard fence. Some woodworkers prefer a fence of solid stock. After the fence has been used for a while, it will become damaged whether it is made of particleboard or solid stock.

Some fences are just a simple piece of wood that clamps between the table board, while others serve a specific function. (See Illus. 7-14.)

Illus. 7-14. *The typical fence is made of either particleboard or solid stock. It clamps between the table boards.*

The most common fence used on a radial arm saw is ¾ inch thick and wide enough to be about ¾ to 1 inch above the front table.

The fence shown in Illus. 7-15, which has a handle, can be used to hold small pieces when you are crosscutting. It allows you to keep your hand clear of the blade, yet maintain control of the workpiece. This makes it much safer to crosscut small parts.

A shaping or horizontal dado fence is somewhat thicker than a regular fence. This extra thickness allows the top edge of a shaping fence to be bevelled for the commercial hold-down tracks. You must cut a dado in the shaper fence to accommodate the shaper or dado head and guard. If a thicker fence cannot be clamped between the table boards, cut a rabbet on the bottom edge of the fence so that it is the thickness of a normal fence.

If you plan to make a hold-down fence, as shown in Illus. 7-16, study the drawing in Illus. 7-17 carefully. Modify the dimensions (if necessary) to fit your saw. Plan your operations in sequence, so that the fence can be made safely and easily.

Begin by cutting the fence to its rectangular shape. Lay out the arc, but do not cut it yet. Now, cut the handle to its rectangular shape and lay out the curves. Do not cut these curves either.

Set up the dado head to cut the grooves in the fence. Mark the position of the grooves on the end of the fence. (See Illus. 7-18.) This will make setup much easier and faster. After all the grooves are cut, set the piece aside for later scrollwork, which is irregular cuts usually made with a scroll, band, or sabre saw. (See Illus. 7-19.)

While the dado head is set up, cut the protrusion on the handle. This is done in the crosscut mode. Note that this protrusion is not centered. This means that two separate height adjustments

Illus. 7-15. This fence-and-handle combination makes crosscutting safer because your hands are clear of the blade when cutting smaller pieces.

Illus. 7-16. This hold-down fence uses a handle that engages with the grooves in the fence to hold your work securely while crosscutting. It also allows your hands to remain clear of the blade.

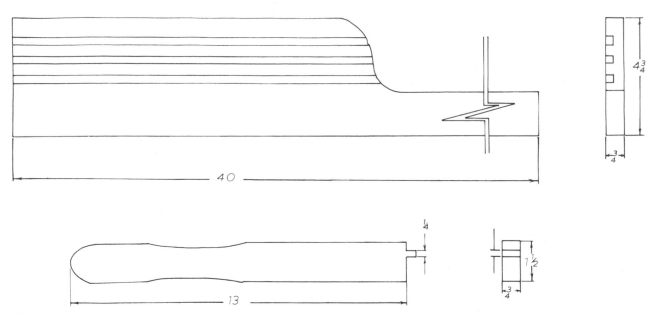

Illus. 7-17. *Study this drawing carefully before making the fence and handle. Note that the protrusion on the handle is not centered.*

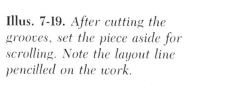

Illus. 7-18. *Mark the grooves on the end of the fence before you begin. This will make the setup much easier.*

Illus. 7-19. *After cutting the grooves, set the piece aside for scrolling. Note the layout line pencilled on the work.*

must be made when you are making the dado cuts. The offset protrusion makes the hold-down device more versatile.

By using different grooves in the fence and by turning the handle over, you can use the fence on just about any stock thickness. If the protrusion were in the middle of the handle, the jig would not be as versatile.

Use a sabre, scroll, or band saw to cut the scrollwork (irregular shapes) on the fence and handle. Leave the layout line, so that you can sand it away using a disc- or spindle-sanding attachment. After the fence and handle are smooth, round over the handle by using a router and a roundover bit. This will make it more comfortable to use.

Clamp the fence between the table boards, being careful to line it up in relation to the blade and motor. The high side of the fence will not allow the motor to clear. Clamp the fence securely. This will prevent the fence from lifting as you exert force on the hold-down handle. It may also be necessary to screw the fence to the front table if the table clamps do not hold securely. Be sure to test the clamps before you actually use the front table.

When doing production crosscutting, remember to allow for sawdust accumulation. A groove cut in the fence at the table level will keep the sawdust from affecting the accuracy of the cut. The groove will have to be cleaned periodically, but not as frequently as a saw with a solid fence.

Arm Stop or Clamp

An arm stop or clamp is another useful accessory for your radial arm saw. Bolt the wooden stop to the arm to control the travel of the carriage. (See Illus. 7-20.) It allows you to cut blind dadoes accurately. (Blind dadoes do not go completely from end to end or from edge to edge.) It also controls the stroke on repetitive cuts. By limiting the stroke, you always know where the blade will be. This can minimize the chance of error or accident.

To make an arm stop, select two pieces of hardwood about 1½ inches thick and about 4

Illus. 7-20. *This arm stop bolts to the saw's arm to control the stroke of the carriage. It is useful for blind dadoes and repetitive cuts.*

inches wider than the arm at its widest point. Clamp the two pieces together and drill two holes to accommodate the hex-head clamping bolts. Drive T-shaped nuts through the holes on one of the pieces with a hammer. Select bolts of the appropriate length, and mount the stop or clamp on the arm. Tighten it securely at the desired setting.

Length Gauge or Stop

When crosscutting, you may frequently find a length gauge or stop to be useful. You can make fine adjustments to the one shown in Illus. 7-21 by turning the flat-head machine screw in or out. Tightening the hex nut against the T-shaped nut locks the adjustment.

To make the length gauge, select a piece of stock about 1 inch square and 10 inches long. Set up the radial arm saw for drilling, and then drill a hole in the middle of one end of the stock. (See Illus. 7-21.) The hole should be about 1½ inches deep and large enough to accommodate the flat-head machine screw. (See Illus. 7-22.)

Drive the T-shaped nut into the wood with a hammer. Thread the machine screw through the hex nut and into the T-shaped nut. (See Illus. 7-23.) The length gauge is now ready for use.

Illus. 7-21. *Use a drilling attachment to drill a hole in the end of the length gauge. The hole should be large enough to accommodate the T-shaped nut. A depth stop is used to get the proper depth of the hole.*

Illus. 7-22. *Make the hole deep enough to accommodate the flat-head machine screw.*

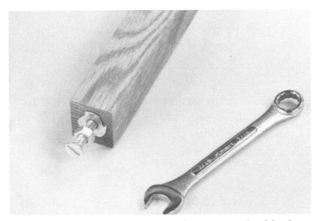

Illus. 7-23. *Drive the T-shaped nut into the block of wood with a hammer. Thread the screw through the hex nut and into the T-shaped nut.*

Mitre Jigs

Mitre jigs are useful for frame work. The advantage of a mitre jig is that it has a 90-degree included angle. This means that all its corners will form a right angle. It also means that the arm of the radial arm saw does not have to be turned. This eliminates any adjustment error.

A flat mitre jig is easy to build. Study Illus. 7-25 first. Modify the dimensions as needed. Begin with a true piece of sheet stock that is at least ½ inch thick. Cut it to the dimensions of the front table on your saw. Attach a cleat to the underside of the sheet on a long edge. (See Illus. 7-26.) This cleat allows the jig to be clamped between the table boards.

Determine the blade's path on the sheet stock. This will dictate the placement of the fences. Note in Illus. 7-24 how the fences are staggered. This keeps the fences from interfering with a mitre on a long piece.

Lay out the position of the fence nearer to the edge of the jig. It should be 45 degrees off the long edge of the jig. Cut the end of the fence as specified and attach it to the sheet stock on the layout line. Cut the other fence as specified and attach it to the sheet stock. Offset it from the first fence. It is important that the second fence be set perpendicular to the first fence. (See Illus. 7-27.)

Illus. 7-24. *The fences on the mitre jig are staggered. This keeps the fences from interfering with the work.*

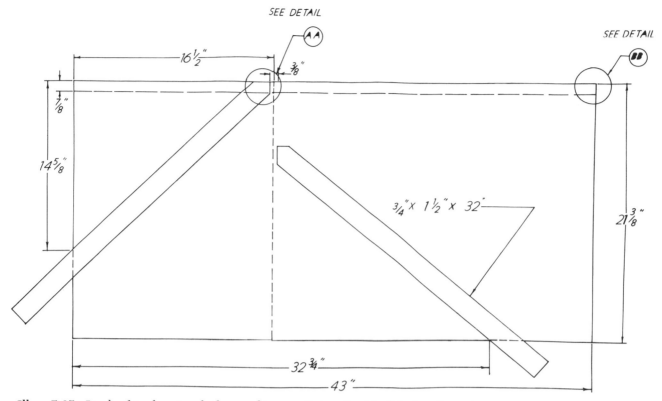

SEE DETAIL

AA

SEE DETAIL

BB

$16\frac{1}{2}"$

$\frac{3}{8}"$

$\frac{7}{8}"$

$14\frac{5}{8}"$

$\frac{3}{4}" \times 1\frac{1}{2}" \times 32"$

$21\frac{3}{8}"$

$32\frac{3}{4}"$

$43"$

Illus. 7-25. *Study this drawing before making a mitring jig. Modify the dimensions to suit your radial arm saw.*

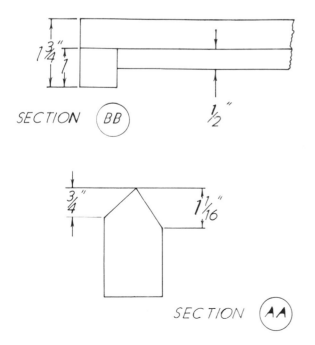

$1\frac{3}{4}"$

$1"$

$\frac{1}{2}"$

SECTION   BB

$\frac{3}{4}"$

$1\frac{1}{16}"$

SECTION   AA

Illus. 7-26. *The details show the cleat placement and the cutting detail for the end of the flat fences.*

Illus. 7-27. *Make sure that the fences have true faces and edges. The fences must also be perpendicular to each other.*

Picture Frames

Picture frames are a particularly useful radial-arm-saw project for beginners because they provide them with the opportunity to cut coves, dadoes, rabbets, and mitres, and also to use the dado head to make frame moulding. Begin with simple frames that require flat mitres. (See Illus. 7-28.) Make sure that you allow enough space in the rabbets for the glass. Make the rabbets as deep as possible. Shallow rabbets may not allow enough room for the photograph, glass, and backing. Allow for the total thickness of these materials.

Use the right-mitre setting to cut stock if both faces are parallel. (See Illus. 7-29–7-32.) Flip the parts over for the mating cut. Use a stop to control the length of the parts.

You can use jigs to help you cut the mitres. Review the section on mitre-cutting in Chapter 5 before beginning. Select a technique that will work with your saw and the available equipment. (See Illus. 7-33.) You may even wish to make the mitre-cutting jigs presented earlier in this chapter. The frames should have tight mitres when assembled. Accurate layout is very important.

Illus. 7-28. *Simple frame profiles with parallel faces and flat mitres are the easiest frames to mitre.*

Illus. 7-29. *Use the right-mitre position for simple frames. Make sure that the setting is accurate.*

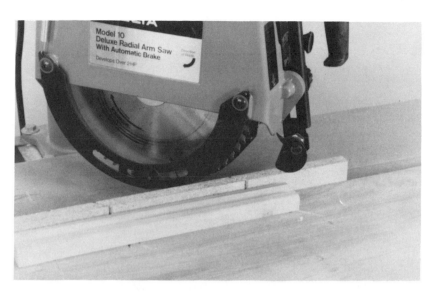

Illus. 7-30. *Position the layout line next to the kerf in the fence. Make sure that the saw blade is in the waste area.*

Illus. 7-31. *Hold the stock securely when making the mitre cut. Pull the carriage (and blade) towards the work. Pull it slowly, to reduce tear-out.*

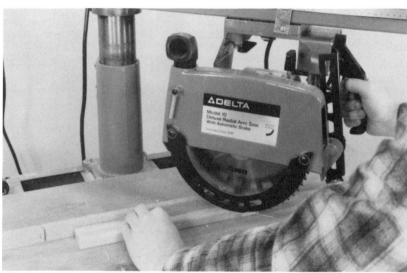

Illus. 7-32. *When the left-mitre position is used, the blade leaves the table. For wide frame stock, attach a table extension.*

Illus. 7-33. *Mitre jigs can be used to cut the mitres. A mitre stop has been clamped to the mitre jig. This stop controls mitre length. The angle is controlled by the jig.*

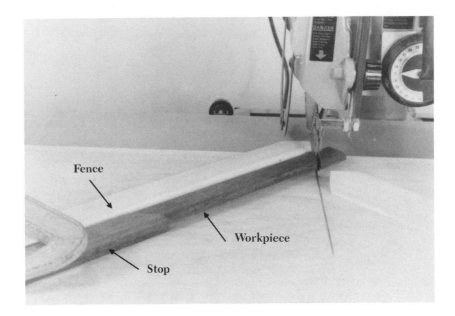

Index

Basics Series

Band Saw Basics
Cabinetry Basics
Radial Arm Saw Basics
Router Basics
Scroll Saw Basics
Sharpening Basics
Table Saw Basics

Other Books by Roger W. Cliffe

Portable Circular-Sawing Machine Techniques
Radial Arm Saw Techniques
Shaper Handbook
Table Saw Basics
Table Saw Techniques
Woodworker's Handbook